Best Practices
for Teaching
SOCIAL STUDIES

Other Corwin Press Books by Randi Stone

Best Practices for Teaching Mathematics: What Award-Winning Classroom Teachers Do, 2007

Best Practices for Teaching Science: What Award-Winning Classroom Teachers Do, 2007

Best Practices for Teaching Writing: What Award-Winning Classroom Teachers Do, 2007

Best Classroom Management Practices for Reaching All Learners: What Award-Winning Classroom Teachers Do, 2005

Best Teaching Practices for Reaching All Learners: What Award-Winning Classroom Teachers Do, 2004

What?! Another New Mandate? What Award-Winning Teachers Do When School Rules Change, 2002

Best Practices for High School Classrooms: What Award-Winning Secondary Teachers Do, 2001

Best Classroom Practices: What Award-Winning Elementary Teachers Do, 1999

New Ways to Teach Using Cable Television: A Step-by-Step Guide, 1997

Best Practices for Teaching

SOCIAL STUDIES

What Award-Winning Classroom Teachers Do

RANDI STONE

CORWIN PRESS
A SAGE Company
Thousand Oaks, CA 91320

For information:

Corwin Press
A SAGE Company
2455 Teller Road
Thousand Oaks, California 91320
www.corwinpress.com

SAGE Ltd.
1 Oliver's Yard
55 City Road
London EC1Y 1SP
United Kingdom

SAGE India Pvt. Ltd.
B 1/I 1 Mohan Cooperative
 Industrial Area
Mathura Road, New Delhi 110 044
India

SAGE Asia-Pacific Pte. Ltd.
33 Pekin Street #02-01
Far East Square
Singapore 048763

Printed in the United States of America.

Library of Congress Cataloging-in-Publication Data

Stone, Randi.
Best practices for teaching social studies: what award-winning classroom teachers do/Randi Stone.
        p. cm.
Includes index.
ISBN 978-1-4129-2452-8 (cloth)
ISBN 978-1-4129-2453-5 (pbk.)
     1. Social sciences—Study and teaching—United States—Case studies. 2. Effective teaching—United States—Case studies. I. Title.

LB1584.S693 2008
300.71'073—dc22   2008001264

This book is printed on acid-free paper.

08   09   10   11   12   10   9   8   7   6   5   4   3   2   1

Acquisitions Editor: Carol Chambers Collins
Editorial Assistants: Gem Rabanera, Brett Ory
Production Editor: Cassandra Margaret Seibel
Copy Editor: Jennifer Withers
Typesetter: C&M Digitals (P) Ltd.
Proofreader: Taryn Bigelow
Indexer: Terri Corry
Cover Designer: Scott Van Atta

Contents

Preface

B *est Practices for Teaching Social Studies* is the fourth book of a five-volume series. The collection includes *Best Practices for Teaching Writing, Best Practices for Teaching Science, Best Practices for Teaching Mathematics*, and *Best Practices for Teaching Reading*. This unique guide provides exemplary teaching practices from award-winning teachers who are willing to share their expertise. These are the teachers we read about in journals and magazines, the teachers who win grants, fellowships, and contests. Enjoy "poking your nose into great classrooms"!

Acknowledgments

Corwin Press acknowledges the important contributions of the following reviewers:

Marian White-Hood
Director of Academics, Principal Support,
    and Accountability
See Forever Foundation
Washington, DC

Laura Lay
Department Chair/Teacher
James River High School, Chesterfield County
Richmond, VA

Peggy Altoff
Past President, NCSS; Social Studies Supervisor
District 11, Colorado Springs
Colorado Springs, CO

Shawn White
Teacher
Weston McEwen High School
Athena, OR

Paul Kelly
Division Head, Social Science/Foreign Language
John Hersey High School
Arlington Heights, IL

Lauren Mittermann
Social Studies Teacher for Grades 7/8
Gibraltar Area Schools
Fish Creek, WI

Lindy G. Poling
Social Studies Department Chair
Millbrook High School
Raleigh, NC

Heather E. Robinson
Fifth-Grade Teacher
Desert Canyon Elementary School
Scottsdale, AZ

About the Author

Randi Stone is a graduate of Clark University, Boston University, and Salem State College. She completed her doctorate in education at the University of Massachusetts, Lowell. She is the author of ten Corwin Press books, including her latest in a series: *Best Practices for Teaching Writing: What Award-Winning Classroom Teachers Do*, *Best Practices for Teaching Mathematics: What Award-Winning Classroom Teachers Do*, and *Best Practices for Teaching Science: What Award-Winning Classroom Teachers Do*. She lives with her teenage daughter, Blair, in Keene, New Hampshire.

About the Contributors

Marguerite Ames, Sixth-Grade Social Studies Teacher
Marion Cross School
22 Church St.
Norwich, VT 05055
School Telephone: (802) 649-1703
E-mail: marguerite.ames@valley.net

Number of Years Teaching: 20
Award: Vermont History Teacher of the Year, 2006

James Wade D'Acosta, Social Studies Teacher
Fairfield Warde High School
755 Melville Ave.
Fairfield, CT 06825
School Telephone: (203) 255-8449
E-mail: jdacosta@fairfield.k12.ct.us

Number of Years Teaching: 18
Awards: Celebration of Excellence Awards by the Connecticut
State Department of Education in Economics and in
American History, 2001 and 1997
Harvard Teachers Prize by the Harvard Club of Southern
Connecticut for inspiring "intellectual curiosity and
the quest for excellence in students," 2000
First National Board Certified Teacher in Adolescence
and Young Adulthood/Social Studies–History in
Connecticut, 1999

Kari Debbink, Seventh- and Eighth-Grade Teacher
Hermosa Montessori Charter School
12051 E. Fort Lowell
Tucson, AZ 85749
School Telephone: (520) 360-3802
E-mail: karidebbink@hotmail.com

Number of Years Teaching: 7
Awards: Toyota Tapestry Grant, 2007
           Captain Planet Foundation Grant, 2006
           Wells Fargo Classroom Grant, 2002

William Fitzhugh, Fifth-Grade Teacher
Reisterstown Elementary School
223 Walgrove Rd.
Reisterstown, MD 21136
School Telephone: (410) 887-1133
E-mail: wfitzhugh@bcps.org

Number of Years Teaching: 35
Awards: NCSS Elementary Social Studies Teacher of the Year, 1997
           NCGE Distinguished Teaching Awards
           Christa McAuliffe Fellowship, 1995

Megan E. Garnett, High School U.S. History Team Leader
Robinson Secondary School
5035 Sideburn Rd.
Fairfax, VA 22032
School Telephone: (703) 426-6928
E-mail: mgarnett@gmu.edu

Number of Years Teaching: 9
Awards: ING Unsung Heroes Award, 2006
           National Education Association Learning and Leadership
             Grant, 2005
           Association of Teacher Educators of Virginia Teacher
             Research Award, 2005

Carol Glanville, First-Grade Teacher
Reynolds Arts Magnet School
235 High St.
Bristol, RI 02809
School Telephone: (401) 254-5987
E-mail: glanvillec@bw.k12.ri.us

Number of Years Teaching: 18
Awards: Wal-Mart Teacher of the Year, Rhode Island, 2002
Milken Educator Award, 1996
Presidential Award for Excellence in Science and Mathematics Teaching, Rhode Island, 1995

Teresa Heinhorst, Social Science High School Teacher
Midwest Central High School
910 S. Washington St.
Manito, IL 61546
School Telephone: (309) 968-6766
E-mail: heinhorst@midwestcentral.org

Number of Years Teaching: 16
Awards: VFW National Citizenship Education Teacher of the Year, 2006
VFW State Citizenship Education Teacher of the Year, Illinois, 2006
Midwest Central Teacher of the Year, 2001

Marsha Mathias, PreK–5 Art Teacher
Sheridan Elementary School
1139 Hillsboro Rd.
Orangeburg, SC 29115
School Telephone: (803) 534-7504
E-mail: mmm18@ocsd5schools.org

Number of Years Teaching: 24
Award: ING Unsung Heroes Award, 2006

Sandra Noel, Physical Education/Health Teacher
Hatch Elementary
1000 N. Ridgeland
Oak Park, IL 60302
School Telephone: (708) 524-3095
E-mail: snoel@op97.org

Number of Years Teaching: 35
Awards: All USA Today Teacher Team, 2006
            Golden Apple, 2006
            Those Who Excel in Illinois, 2002

John Pieper, Fifth-Grade Teacher
Webster Stanley Elementary School
915 Hazel St.
Oshkosh, WI 54901
School Telephone: (920) 424-0460
E-mail: john.pieper@oshkosh.k12.wi.us

Number of Years Teaching: 26
Awards: Teach Vietnam Teachers Network Representative,
            Washington, D.C., 2006
            Japan Fulbright Memorial Fund Participant, 2005
            Disney American Teacher Award Honoree, 2003

Robert Rodey, Advanced Placement U.S. History Teacher
Marian Catholic High School
700 Ashland Ave.
Chicago Heights, IL 60411
School Telephone: (708) 755-7565
E-mail: bobrodey@marianchs.com

Number of Years Teaching: 43
Awards: Golden Apple, 2007
            Gilder Lehrman Institute of American History, History
            Teacher of the Year Illinois State Winner, 2004

Diana Schmiesing, Second-Grade Teacher
Providence Elementary School
3616 Jermantown Rd.
Fairfax, VA 22030
School Telephone: (703) 460-4400
E-mail: diana.schmiesing@fcps.edu

Number of Years Teaching: 25
Awards: USA Today, All USA Teacher Team, 2006
Fairfax County Public School Teacher of the Year Nominee, 2005
Fairfax City Rotary Teacher of the Year, 2005

Monique Wallen, Fifth-Grade Teacher
Sawgrass Elementary
12655 NW 8th St.
Sunrise, FL 33325
School Telephone: (754) 322-8500
E-mail: monique.wallen@browardschools.com

Number of Years Teaching: 10
Awards: Toyota Tapestry Mini-Grant Award Winner, 2007
Broward Education Foundation Grant Winner, 2006 and 2007
Toshiba America Foundation Grant Winner, 2006

In loving memory of my father
George Trachtenberg
Forever a Diamond

PART I

Elementary and Middle School

CHAPTER 1

Celebrating Our Constitution

Diana Schmiesing

Fairfax, Virginia

I follow the tenets of the responsive classroom, which state that children need to feel that their classroom is truly their classroom and not the teacher's. In September when the students arrive, I have few pictures and posters up on the walls. I want the classroom to reflect student's ideas. I have a blank bulletin board with the title, "Hopes and Dreams for Second Grade" (idea published in *The First Six Weeks of School* by Paula Denton and Roxann Kriete).

For the first few weeks, the students explore the classroom and get to know me, and I establish routines and procedures. We discuss their hopes and dreams pertaining to second grade. The students then write and illustrate their ideas. To conclude the lesson, students "buddy up" and share their feelings. During morning meeting, students then share their hopes and dreams with the class. Then I lead a discussion on how we can fulfill their wishes. Through this guided discussion, the children realize that we need to establish some rules.

For homework, the children must write a classroom rule. I send home a 5 × 7-inch file card with this explanation:

> We have been discussing our hopes and dreams for second grade and realize we need some rules so everyone can achieve their wishes. Tonight's assignment for your favorite second grader is for him or her to write a classroom rule, and illustrate a student following that rule.

The following day, each student brings in his or her file card and shares the rule that he or she feels is important for the classroom. A sample rule is "Don't run in the classroom." I may ask what they think we should do instead of running. We establish "We should walk in the classroom to be safe." We sort their rules into three main categories:

1. Respect your classroom and school.

2. Respect others.

3. Respect yourself.

We decide where we should place each card. It is fairly easy to place any of their rules into one of the three categories. I then ask the students if they are willing to sign a document stating that they agree to these rules. This lesson teaches students about the rights and responsibilities of a citizen and the need for the Constitution. Students discuss the historical context of events leading up to the signing of the Constitution and write "laws" for the classroom, which we develop into a class constitution.

The lesson leads to the celebration of Constitution Day, on or close to September 17 (the official date was September 17, 1787). On our constitution day, I devote a special area in the class for U.S.A. decorations and a special "signing table." When children enter the classroom, I write the following on the board: "Today is a special day! We will be signing our class constitution. Does anyone know what might have happened years ago?" The children can "check in" by putting a response on a paper chart.

Of course, most children will guess that the event of long ago was the signing of the Constitution. We make a KWL chart (what we know, what we want to know, and what we have learned). Some points made are as follows:

- The founding fathers put themselves at risk so we could be an independent country.
- The founding fathers recognized a need for strong laws.
- The founding fathers did not want to have a king or one person in charge, so they came up with three branches of government.

I ask children to step back in time. I hand them a copy of the painting *Scene at the Signing of the Constitution of the United States* by Howard Chandler Christy. Each student is also given a "Picture Detective Sheet" to complete after looking at the painting. I then tell the children that this is when they have a chance to become one of the characters in the picture. The front of the room becomes the stage; some of the students perform and some are in the audience. I spend time discussing how actors perform and how audiences respond. When children clearly understand the expectations of this activity, I rarely get any silly behavior.

I tell the children that when they come onto the stage, they can imagine what their person was doing before the painting "froze" them in time. When I say "Freeze," they must strike the pose exactly like the person in the picture. I tell the audience that when I say "Curtain's going up," they must be quiet and watch the performance. They look for clues to figure out what characters their classmates are playing. I do not say that everyone has to choose a different person, so I might end up with six George Washingtons! This could lead to a wonderful discussion on why all six chose Washington. Here are ten guiding questions for this activity:

1. Does your character look very important?

2. Did you choose him because you know who he is?

3. Why do you think he is facing the people?

4. Do you think the painter of the picture purposely put the desk and Washington on a different level?

5. Do you know who this person is? What do you know about him?

6. Does the picture let you know where the people are?

7. Do you see any women? Why do you think there weren't any?

8. Why do you think some people are raising their hands?

9. Does this picture tell you what is happening? What do you think the man by the table is doing?

10. Do you see any important symbols or people in the picture? How do you know they are important?

The student performances are wonderful. Their attention to detail is extraordinary. History comes alive! At the conclusion of the lesson, students sign their own classroom constitution. They see a copy of our real Constitution, and we discuss those first important words: *We the People*.

CHAPTER 2

Investigating Historical Objects and Pictures

Diana Schmiesing

Fairfax, Virginia

I n this hands-on lesson for second graders, students learn how and why communities change over time. Students will be able to

- Look at various "antique" objects, discuss their possible uses, and compare and contrast them with similar current-day objects
- Discuss the reasons the objects have changed or why they are no longer used

The books *Homeplace* by Anne Shelby and *The Little House* by Virginia Lee Burton are excellent resources showing how a community changes. While reading each book to the children, I ask them to be "detectives" and find changes that they see from the beginning to the end of each book. I chart each book and record some of the student's responses. We discuss the possible reasons for the changes.

I ask my students to think about their lives growing up compared to their parents' lives. I also share how my childhood was different from theirs. We discuss how and why they are different. I then distribute different "artifacts" that I find in antique stores. Some of the items are typewriters, telephones, radios, and washboards. This lesson can work using photos, but it works best with real objects.

The students form groups and are given one "antique" to examine. I ask them to look carefully at their "artifacts." They, as "detectives," find clues (serial numbers, dates). To spark their curiosity, I put each object in a covered box and wheel them into the classroom on a cart. The students are enthusiastic when they discover their assigned "artifact."

I ask the following questions:

1. What have you discovered?

2. What do you think this object was used for?

3. Would we still need this object today? Why or why not?

4. Do we have something like this today?

5. How do objects change over time (for example, a cell phone, a washing machine)?

After our class discussion, students use their creativity to draw objects of the future. Are there "undiscovered" resources? We discuss why things may change.

CHAPTER 3

Tasting

A Cultural and Culinary Journey to Italy

Sandra Noel

Oak Park, Illinois

I n this tasting lesson, we combine social studies with science. Students develop social skills, creativity, and cross-cultural knowledge. As part of the social studies multidisciplinary curriculum, "Tastings" allows students to appreciate the environment, culture, and cuisine of many countries. My goal is for students to connect with nature. We travel the continents, and each week wide-eyed second graders ask, "Where are we going this week?" During a recent "trip" to Mexico, one student commented, "This is better than TV!" and another responded, "This is better than school!"

📸 Learning Outcomes

Children will be able to

- Identify Italy on the globe
- Recognize Italy as part of the continent of Europe

- Describe the climate of Italy
- Name one plant grown in the country for food
- Appreciate the cultural connection to food
- Describe the "greet and eat" customs and courtesies of the culture
- Name one nutrient found in the food
- Describe the food using their five senses (taste, texture, appearance, sounds, smell)
- Name a famous Italian artist
- Name a famous landmark

▨ Materials Needed

- Recipes (Caprese salad, white bean bruschetta)
- One sample of each raw ingredient (tomato, olive oil, basil, mozzarella, beans)
- Globe or map
- Italian flag
- Plates, forks, and napkins for each child
- Paper, watercolors, and brushes for each child
- Luciano Pavarotti CD with CD player
- Pinocchio books and puppets
- Posters of the Leaning Tower of Pisa, the Sistine Chapel, Michelangelo, Ponte Vecchio, the Colosseum

Station 1 can be a long table to display the globe, flag, and other cultural art, artifacts, and architecture.

Station 2 is best set up as a "U" shape of desks or tables with a display table in the center. Students sit on the outside of the U, facing the center table. Each student's place is set with a serving of the food to taste.

Station 3 can be desks set up with paper taped to the underside of the desk, brushes, and watercolors.

Station 4 is set up with books and pictures from *Pinocchio*.

Station 5 is a listening station with the CD player and Pavarotti CD.

I. Soil (a discussion of the environment and climate)

A. Italy is a country of microclimates. There are 20 distinct regions in Italy. Because the country is a peninsula and because much of it is mountainous, the climate varies greatly from region to region. In the south and along the coasts, the weather is mild, while in the north and the more mountainous regions, the temperatures can get quite cold.

B. Many different crops are grown in Italy because of its climactic variation. Sheep and goats roam the mountains, so goat's and sheep's milk cheeses are common. Butter is also common. Olive trees are grown in the mild southern climates, so olive oil is very common throughout the southern and central regions. Tomatoes need a warm climate and were introduced to Italy by the Spanish, who brought them back from their explorations of South and Central America.

C. Due to its many ports in the Mediterranean Sea, for centuries, Italy has been a trading center. For that reason, the cuisine has adopted and adapted spices and cooking techniques from other parts of the world (for example, noodles and rice from China, coffee from Turkey, spices from all over the world).

D. To much of Italy, olives and olive oil are very important crops. Olives are grown on trees. The trees become twisted and hollow over time and can survive through anything except cold. They can even tolerate fire. Olives blossom from white flowers on the trees, like apples, and are harvested when it is warm (from November to March) each year. The olives are beaten from trees with poles, are removed with branch-shaker machines, or are collected from the ground. There are hundreds of different types of olives, and they are picked either green or black. The green are not fully ripe. To make oil, fresh-picked olives are rushed to mills, where they are pressed the day of harvest. Four different types of oil are produced based on how much heat is used to extract the oil.

II. Roots (the culture and cultural relationship to food)

A. Traditionally, Italians enjoy a slower-paced lifestyle than many other countries, taking time to socialize with family and friends.

B. Most Italians still eat their main meal in the middle of the day. At 1:00 p.m., most businesses and schools close. Children and parents come home to enjoy a leisurely, one- to two-hour main meal together. Often, grandparents and other extended family join too. Most people return to school or work for a few hours after the main meal. A light snack at 5:00 p.m. is common. Dinner is served late in the evening (8:00 or 9:00 p.m.).

C. Eating is a time for socializing, and any celebration is accompanied by a feast. When an adult has a birthday, it is customary for him or her to take friends out for dinner.

D. Italians do not, as a whole, eat fast food. Italy is the heart of the Slow Food Movement, which encourages people to savor food local to the region.

E. Italians take food very seriously. Many strictly enforced laws govern artisanal processes of food production.

F. Supermarkets only exist in major Italian cities. Most Italians purchase seasonal and local products from weekly markets (like a farmer's market) or from sellers who produce their foodstuffs nearby and come through towns with carts.

G. Many Italian foods resemble the Italian flag:

> Red—tomatoes used in sauces, pastas, and marinaras
>
> White—garlic and mozzarella cheese
>
> Green—Italian herbs like oregano, basil, and parsley

H. Fun fact: The Italians were the first to use a fork!

III. Stem (nutrition and health)

A. Tomatoes (like many other red fruits) contain:

1. Vitamin C, which helps us heal when we are sick (pantomime pneumonic "a-choo")

2. Antioxidants. Tomatoes are a native plant of Peru. When they were brought to Europe in the mid-1500s, Europeans were reluctant to eat them because they are a plant of the nightshade family and many nightshades are highly poisonous. It turns out the tomato contains many antioxidants (especially lycopene), which protect the tomato plant from pests and also protect our bodies from germs and from cancer.

B. Olive oil contains:

    1. Antioxidants, which help keep our cells healthy and help us fight germs

    2. Monounsaturated fat ("good" fat), which keeps our heart healthy

C. Basil (like many green things) contains:

    1. Folate
       a. Sounds like the word "foliage," which is also green
       b. Helps cells to grow

D. Mozzarella cheese contains:

    1. Calcium
       a. Helps make strong bones
       b. Helps make strong teeth (have students smile at each other and wiggle their phalanges)

LESSON OUTLINE

Station 1: "Greet" (props: globe, map with stars to indicate countries traveled)

1. Simple greeting

    Formally, for most of the day: *Buon giorno* ("good day")

    Informally: *Ciao*! ("hello" and "goodbye")

2. Continent song

3. "Where are we today?"

    Point out country on map and globe.

    Discuss geography and how it affects climate, trade, and what the people can grow.

    What is the climate like?

    What do the people eat?

    How does the food grow?

4. "Who are the Italians?"

Discuss the culture and its relationship to food.

What are the cultural relationships and rituals surrounding food (for example, value of locally available foods, time of meals, religious beliefs associated with food)?

Describe any ritual done prior to eating (for example, *Buon appetito*).

When do the people eat their main meal?

Where do they typically eat?

Station 2: "Eat" (props: raw food ingredients, charts)

5. "What are we eating today?"

Show the raw ingredients that are being tasted.

Discuss the way they are grown and harvested.

Discuss the nutrients contained in each and how they benefit the body.

Remind students of "no yuck" policy.

Ask children why this is a necessary policy.

Reasons: not instructive; we don't learn from yuck or yum

A way of communicating this:

How many of you like raw tomatoes?

How many of you like spaghetti sauce?

If we just said yuck to all tomatoes, we would miss out on some of our favorite things. You might like the way something looks, but not the way it feels in your mouth, and so forth.

6. *Buon appetito!*—"Good appetite." "Enjoy!"

Walk students, step-by-step, through tasting all of the ingredients. (Instructor will need to have a sample plate.)

"Exploring the rainbow with all senses."

Start using your senses from the top of the body with the first color of the rainbow:

Pick up the red food:

Sight

Let's look at the food. (Teacher holds the whole/raw ingredient.)

Describe its color. Is it the same on the inside as on the outside? Is it shiny or dull?

Sound

Does it make a sound when you tap it? Can you shake it to make a noise? Does it have a coating that makes a sound? Does it make a sound when you break it in half? Can you tell if it's ripe by checking the sound?

Smell

What does it smell like? Does it smell like something else that you are familiar with?

Touch

Describe the texture. Is it smooth, bumpy, rough? Does it feel cold or warm? Is it the same on the inside as on the outside?

Taste

Ask children to touch it to the tip of their tongue only. This is where the sweet receptors are located. Does it taste sweet?

Now, crunch down on it. Does it taste different? For some foods (like cherry tomatoes), all of the taste will be on the inside. Reiterate the importance of full exploration of food.

Does the food taste different with your whole mouth?

Mouth feel

How does it feel in your mouth? Is it crunchy, squishy, gooey, juicy, soft, or hard?

Nutrition information

Sensory analysis: How many students tried something new? How many liked the colors, taste, and so forth?

Station 3: A Modern Michelangelo (pictures of Sistine Chapel)

7. Explain that Michelangelo lived from 1475 to 1564 and was a sculptor, architect, and painter. Show a picture of the Sistine Chapel and explain that he painted the scenes while on his back.

   Instruct the students to get a brush and watercolors and find a place under a desk or bench and begin painting as Michelangelo.

Station 4: The Adventures of Pinocchio (books, puppets)

8. Tell the students that *Pinocchio* was written by Italian author Carlo Collodi in 1881 and is a classic in children's literature.

   Explain that the students are to dramatize or act out the story at this station.

Station 5: Italy—Home of Opera

9. Instruct the students that Italians are proud of their artistic heritage and that Italian composers include Rossini, Verdi, and Puccini. Most Italians have a firm knowledge of opera and attend performances whenever possible.

   Have the students listen to a Luciano Pavarotti CD. Explain that he was a famous Italian tenor.

Reflection

After visiting Stations 1 and 2 together and rotating through Stations 3 through 5, bring the students together and have them tell a friend one thing they learned about Italy. Send the recipes home with the students and ask them to share the Slow Food philosophy with their families and go out and play the game of Italy—soccer.

Recipes

Insalata Caprese (Caprese Salad)

2 large tomatoes, sliced

½ pound fresh mozzarella, drained and sliced

12 fresh basil leaves

3 tablespoons olive oil

2 tablespoons balsamic vinegar

Salt and pepper to taste

Place a slice of tomato on a platter. Place a slice of mozzarella on the platter, overlapping about half the tomato. Place a basil leaf on the platter, overlapping about half the mozzarella.

Repeat alternating layers, until all slices are used.

In a small bowl, whisk oil and vinegar together. Pour over salad. Season to taste with salt and pepper.

Makes 4 to 6 servings.

White Bean Bruschetta

4 cans white beans, drained

20 sun-dried tomatoes packed in olive oil, thinly sliced

4 to 6 sage leaves, cut into thin strips

3 to 4 cloves garlic, minced

Olive oil

Toasted Italian bread, thinly sliced

Sauté 2 tablespoons olive oil, 3 to 4 cloves minced garlic, and sage leaf strips.

Pour into Tupperware-type container and add ½ cup olive oil.

On day of serving, add 4 cans of beans and thinly sliced sun-dried tomatoes to mixture.

Combine mixture and mash.

Serve on bread.

Makes 20 to 30 servings.

CHAPTER 4

A Tale of a Whale

John Pieper

Oshkosh, Wisconsin

F inding the time to adequately cover a topic is a frequent complaint of teachers when trying to structure lessons around the required standards and benchmarks. This integrated unit on whaling incorporates elements of history, economics, geography, reading, math, writing, technology, and even some science.

▧ Procedures and Goals

Show a five- to ten-minute clip from the movie *Moby Dick*. Ask the students to take five to ten minutes to individually write down what they saw, and then what they know about whales or whaling. Divide the class into small groups. Students will share within their groups what they wrote down. After everyone has had the opportunity to share, the groups should continue to brainstorm on the topic of whales. One person in each group should record the responses. Collect the responses and use this information to determine what the students already know. Goals are as follows:

- Demonstrate an ability to use map skills to plot latitude and longitude on a world map.
- Collect and report on the economics associated with whales from 1800 to the present.
- Develop an understanding of how the value of a resource may change over time.
- Support a viewpoint in writing and/or in a debate.
- Apply technology skills to research and report on whales and whaling.
- Compare and contrast fictional accounts of whaling to nonfictional sources.

🐋 Resources and Materials

The film *Moby Dick* (1998 or 1956)

Herman Melville's books *Moby Dick* and *Two Years Before the Mast*

Wikipedia Web site

The Web book *You Wouldn't Want to Sail on the Whaling Ship Essex!* (www.salariya.com)

Web search topics: whales, Greenpeace, whale sightseeing tours, modern-day whale hunting

Large world map

12 × 17-inch outline map of the world

🐋 Steps for the Teacher

1. Create groups of six students. Each group will become a ship's crew.

2. Provide each crew with a grading rubric. A captain may be elected for each ship, and tasks assigned.

3. Schedule enough time for the students to explore the various Web sites.

4. If the students are not familiar with how to conduct a debate, provide lessons and practice prior to having one.

5. Read selected passages aloud from Herman Melville's novel *Moby Dick*.

6. Monitor student progress on activities.

7. Assess student achievement based on group work and individual performance.

8. Share products with parents and other classes.

Student Responsibilities

- Work within the group to complete as much of "the voyage" as possible.
- Prepare and participate in a debate on the pros and cons of modern-day whaling.
- Turn assignments in on time.
- Complete a written reflection demonstrating learning.

Group Work Requirement Rubric

1. Identify the different types of whales and indicate which ones were hunted for oil.

2. Describe what life on a whaling ship was like. Include information on how the whales were caught, how the blubber was made into oil, and what other products were produced from whales.

3. What factors led to the decline of whaling in the nineteenth century?

4. How much was the whale oil worth?

5. Produce a brochure or flier for an imaginary whale-watching company. The flier or brochure will be based on information from actual whale-watching companies. Include the location of

the tour, how much the tour costs, and what is included in a tour package.

6. Prepare and participate in a debate on the subject of modern-day whaling.

7. Create a skit that would demonstrate what it was like to hunt whales.

8. If weather permits, small groups of students can use meter-sticks or yardsticks and chalk to physically measure the lengths of the whales on the playground. Measuring the lengths in a hallway is an additional option. String may be substituted for chalk.

9. Read or listen to selected excerpts from *Moby Dick.*

10. Read *You Wouldn't Want to Sail on the Whaling Ship Essex!*

11. Present your group's work to the class.

12. Complete an assessment in which each member of the group writes a reflection on what was learned in the unit.

Helpful Tips

- Provide the structure and time for the students to work, but give them the opportunity to complete the tasks on their own.
- Try to devote at least two weeks to this unit. The integrated concept should free up time for the students to complete the various activities.
- Fifth-grade students are fully capable of engaging in a debate. The unit lends itself well to addressing the individual abilities and needs of the students.

CHAPTER 5

The Art of Social Studies/The Social Studies in Art

William Fitzhugh

Reisterstown, Maryland

A s a geographer interested in the development of culture, I have always thought that a society's culture arises from people's interaction with their physical environment. Clothing, food, and shelter reflect a society's adaptations to its physical surroundings. Societies also express themselves through art, using the materials found in their environment. I have integrated the art activities that follow in my teaching.

⌘ Australia: Aboriginal Painting

The Aborigines of Australia painted on bark and rock face to create their traditional artwork. To simulate this, children paint large Australian animals on craft paper that we paint with earth colors to represent the bark and rock found in nature. When the paper dries, children dip straws in paint and make dot-like designs on their painting to trace the outline and features of their animals. Many of the animals used in traditional art refer back to events that occurred long ago in the history of Australia. The past history is called the "Dream Time." It's the time when the pattern of Aboriginal life was established thousands of years ago.

▧   Russia: Icons

Icons are religious art of old Russia. Byzantine artists also produced wonderful icons. The subject matter is usually religious: Christ, angels, apostles, or Old Testament heroes. The images have halos. In our schoolwork, students use a black marker to draw the scene. The picture is then colored with bright crayons. The finished piece is coated with shellac, which gives it not only a glow, but an antiqued look as well. Aluminum foil can be cut out and used for halos. Aluminum foil is difficult to cut. Orange shellac makes aluminum foil look like gold and gives an even more antiqued look to the icon. A silver or gold paint marker can be used to give a halo effect.

▧   China: Calligraphy

Use a 20 × 18-inch strip of white paper. Dampen the paper first with a wet sponge. Students paint a seasonal picture in the top left quarter using watercolors. Then let the paper dry. While the painting is drying, children write their names in cursive letters going vertically down the paper. They need to practice this several times or they can practice copying traditional Chinese word-images. They also need time to practice writing strokes with a brush. I use watered-down black tempera paint. Giving students practice writing the script and controlling the brush helps them achieve a more pleasing finished product. Then children vertically paint their names in calligraphy onto their dried seasonal painting in the right bottom quarter. After the painting dries, it can be rolled up. Dowels can be glued to the top and bottom of the scroll.

Mexico: *Ojo de Dios* (God's Eye)

There is a tribe in Mexico that makes the God's Eye. They are the Huichol people. Legend has it that the *Ojo de Dios* is like a wand that allows us to see and understand the unknown. God's Eyes bring health and long life. Craft sticks are glued at right angles. The yarn is wound around the stick and across to the next stick. Yarn can cover the sticks over the top of the stick or under the bottom of the stick. Colors of yarn can be changed easily. Feathers and beads can be added to the finished weaving.

Japan: Wood Block Prints

We print these on traditional rice paper, which is not really made from rice. This gives a more authentic look to the finished print. The students make blocks out of Styrofoam and use tempera paint instead of printer's ink. This dries faster. In Japan, illustrations are traditionally drawn on paper first. Students need to decide on a finished illustration before beginning to make their Styrofoam block. The picture is transferred to a block and cut out. Each color of the print requires its own block. Traditionally, four colors are used in compiling the finished print. I use two-color prints with students. Each color needs to dry before printing the next color.

Africa: Kente Cloth

We print on brown craft paper. The paper is folded to give three-inch squares. Each student makes a small print block. Students can print their block in the squares to make a design and share one another's blocks to make the complete design more interesting. Draw a geometric design onto a three-inch piece of cardboard. Use white glue to trace the pattern. After the glue dries, the raised surface becomes the surface to be inked and printed. The block is printed on the folded paper in a predetermined sequence. Repeating the sequence is part of the process.

CHAPTER 6

Assembly-Line Lunches

Kari Debbink

Tucson, Arizona

In this lesson, students learn about factory conditions and processes during the Industrial Revolution by engaging in a hands-on activity with the potential to benefit the community. We donate the lunches made during this lesson to a local homeless shelter. If you will be donating the food you prepare, you may want to alter the ingredients according to the preferences of the recipient.

Materials*

Paper lunch bags	Several loaves of bread
2 jars of peanut butter	Lunch meat, turkey, or ham (or other)
2 jars of jelly	
2 squeeze bottles of mustard	2 jars of mayonnaise

Presliced cheese	Napkins
Bags of apples or oranges	Fold-and-close sandwich bags
Fun-size bags of chips	Plastic knives

*Materials will vary depending on how you adapt this lesson. Be aware that peanut allergies are common!

Procedures

1. Find a shelter or other institution that accepts donated lunches. Note the requirements for the contents of their lunches. Modify the materials list accordingly. Also determine how the lunches will be delivered.

2. Divide students into two groups, Factory A and Factory B. Set up two rows of tables so each factory has a long workspace. Students create an assembly line to make lunches (one student puts peanut butter on the bread and passes it to the next student, who puts on jelly and closes the sandwich; that student passes it to the next person, who puts it into a plastic bag, and so on). One factory makes peanut butter and jelly sandwiches, and the other makes meat sandwiches. The two factories compete to see who can first meet their lunch quota (which is decided ahead of time). Set up materials at each factory station.

3. Explain these directions to both factories:
   A. You are factories producing lunches. Your job is to make 50 (or your established quota) lunches as fast as you can. The faster you work, the more profit for your factory. Your job is to make your sandwiches faster than your competitor (the other factory).
   B. Each lunch must contain one peanut butter and jelly sandwich or one meat and cheese sandwich (with mustard and mayonnaise), one piece of fruit, one bag of chips, and one napkin.
   C. You must also consider quality because buyers do not purchase messy lunches.

D. You must work in silence. Any talking results in time lost from production, and this is each factory's number one priority. Factory workers may be fired for talking (taken out of the game—leaving fewer factory workers to accomplish the goal).

E. You will be given a few minutes to work out the most efficient methods of division of labor within your factory groups. When I say "Go," start producing lunches as quickly as possible.

4. Give the two factories a few minutes to determine who is going to do each job and in what order they want to proceed. You can suggest efficient ways to work, or you can leave it completely up to them. Have all of the students wash their hands!

5. Say "Go!" to begin production. Stand between the groups and monitor them for talking and for quality control. If you see a lunch violating quality control, wait until the entire lunch is made and confiscate it. You can decide to take away a lunch for many reasons. Some might include oozing peanut butter, jelly, mayonnaise, or mustard; an uneven layout of items on the bread; protruding sandwich meat; and ripped or torn paper bags.

6. Each factory is responsible for keeping an accurate count of its lunches. When you think your factory has 50 lunches, say "Done," and the inspector will count your lunches. If you have less than 50, you will lose five of your finished lunches, and the game will continue. If you have 50 lunches or more, your factory wins! Students then fix any lunches that were confiscated so they are ready for the shelter.

▧ Follow-Up Questions

1. How did you feel while participating in this activity?

2. Why did people work in factories during the Industrial Revolution?

3. What were the conditions in the factories during the Industrial Revolution?

4. What were the concerns of the factory workers during these times?

5. How do you feel about the factory inspector? What do you think would happen if you stood up to the inspector?

6. How do you think factory conditions are today?

7. Why did you think the assembly line became widely used?

8. Do you think it would be faster if factory workers made lunches individually?

Helpful Tips

- Our students read *Lyddie* by Katherine Paterson or *The Jungle* by Upton Sinclair during this unit.
- This activity is done best with groups of at least 14, preferably 18. Larger groups will also work. You can always have more factories or the jobs can become more specialized. This lesson should take approximately one hour, depending on the discussion time.
- Review the assembly-line and mass-production process prior to beginning the activity.
- Arrange the tables before you explain the activity because they can take about ten minutes to set up.
- Make sure you cover the tables and don't do this on carpet because it can get very messy!
- Make sure students wash their hands prior to touching any food.
- Fire anyone who talks or complains because it will make discussions more lively.
- Be picky about quality. Confiscate several lunches.
- To show how assembly lines are more efficient, you could have a third factory (especially for a large group) where each person makes complete lunches himself or herself instead of specializing in one area.

CHAPTER 7

The History Kids

Celebrating Our Local Heritage

Carol Glanville

Bristol, Rhode Island

During my last period on Fridays, 21 students enter a time warp. The students submerge themselves in the past. These are the History Kids, whose community service mission is to help our local historical societies and museums preserve our local heritage. On Fridays, you will find them reading research, learning historic dances, memorizing parts for dramatized historic events, practicing needle-work, or copying famous documents onto vellum with quill and ink. They can be found rewriting plays, learning historic games, and listening to folktale or factual stories about their hometown.

This past holiday season, the History Kids wowed their community with their knowledge when they took over the first shift of tours at the grand old federal mansion Linden Place. The students dressed in period costumes and were assigned to various rooms. They were each given some pages of the tour guide's script and read them to visitors. Most of the children memorized their parts. Fourth and fifth graders explained the Triangular Trade and the economic dependence on this trade that led to the town's bankruptcy in 1825. These are vague concepts and often are not very meaningful even for secondary students. But for History Kids, the events in books come alive. The script began with the privateers of the eighteenth century; included Revolutionary War participants, slave traders, and Industrial Revolution manufacturers; and ended with the Barrymores of the twentieth century. These History Kids have a strong understanding of the major events that formed our United States. Their innocent puzzlement is a metaphor for so much American history: "When you see how beautiful this mansion is and you want to preserve it, but know it was built from slavery, it makes your heart ache."

The History Kids were asked by the Town Council to help establish a Founders Day, and they did this by performing skits based on the proprietors' laying out the Town of Bristol from the lands of the Wampanoag in 1680. They learned about the King Philip War that was started right here. They learned about the businessmen whose names are on so many of our schools and roads. They learned about Roger Williams. The children's parents learned about King Philip, the founding fathers, and Roger Williams. This is the sixth year of History Kids, and the following is our plan of the organization of heterogeneous groups.

▨ First Year

Students learn all about the toys and games that were played before electricity, such as cat's cradle, cup and ball (great for kindergarten and first grade), marbles, hoop rolling, tippy, graces, jacks, checkers, chess, paper dolls, and card games.

▨ Second Year

Students begin to learn more difficult games. They are given multiple-choice history questions to memorize and deliver in performances. (Adult audiences love these local history trivia games.) They have costumes and parts in our plays, tours, and demonstrations.

🗞 Third Year

Students branch into a specialty. They have the opportunity to learn embroidery or hoop rolling. There are students who become experts on the slave trade. Others become knowledgeable about our town in the Civil War. (We have two siblings participating in the History Kids program who, with their father, reenact the Civil War and occasionally travel on weekends, performing as historic figures!)

Rhode Island was the first state to declare its independence from Britain. This happened on May 4, 1776. The History Kids were asked by Governor and Mrs. Carcieri to be a part of a celebration. We practiced how to handle a buffet table, use a punch ladle, and make introductions and small talk. We also brushed up on our Rhode Island history. The History Kids were also asked to assist the Chamber of Commerce and the Governor with the Statehouse kickoff of a new tourism program. The veteran History Kids and a veteran parent volunteer did it all. We have many veteran parent volunteers who know the ropes and enjoy learning local history along with their children.

CHAPTER 8

Who Would You Help?

Kari Debbink

Tucson, Arizona

E xplain to your students that they will be participating in a simulation. The class will act as an organization responsible for distributing $5 billion in aid to various problem areas around the world. As members of this organization, they will each submit a proposal to the entire organization on how $1 billion should be spent. After researching his or her chosen area and problem, each organization member (student) creates a presentation focusing on how the organization should spend the money. As a group, the organization will vote on which projects will receive funding.

Procedure

1. The class brainstorms a list of social and environmental problems that need solutions. This gives students a starting point. Books, Web sites, and other resources should be made available.

2. The students choose a specific region and problem within that area. For instance, a student may choose "AIDS education in Rwanda," but not simply "AIDS." Students research why it is so important to fund their cause. In addition, they suggest specific programs and ways to address the problem.

3. Students create a three- to five-minute PowerPoint presentation for the rest of the organization (class) to view. This presentation should reflect their research and explain the problem, urgency to fund, possible ways to combat the problem, and possible improvements that would result from action. Once each student shows his or her presentation, the organization votes on which five causes should receive $1 billion.

Helpful Tips

- This may be a difficult assignment for some students because it is fairly open-ended. It is very important to generate a list of social and environmental problems ahead of time. If students have difficulty generating ideas, help with suggestions.
- If students are unfamiliar with PowerPoint, other presentation options can be selected (posters, collages, speeches).
- You don't have to structure this as a competitive activity. Some students try harder if they know their work will be compared to others'. However, in some classes, it may be best to forgo the competition.
- This activity can be done in groups.
- You may want to show an exemplary presentation ahead of time so students see your expectations.

CHAPTER 9

Exploring Diversity Through Technology

Marsha Mathias

Orangeburg, South Carolina

> *From a multicultural perspective, all students should receive an education that continuously affirms human diversity—one that embraces the history and culture of all racial groups and that teaches people of color to take charge of their own destinies. With regard to teaching, a multicultural perspective assumes that teachers will hold high expectations for all students and that they will challenge those students who are trapped in the cycle of poverty and despair to rise above it.*
>
> C. A. Grant*

---

*From "Desegregation, Racial Attitudes, and Intergroup Contact: A Discussion of Change," by C. A. Grant, 1990, *Phi Delta Kappan*, 72(1), p. 31.

I n a joint venture between the art and social studies departments, we as teachers decided to design a unit of study that would make history more of a reality to our students. We wanted them to realize that what they read in their history books did, in fact, occur, and individual lives were affected by the changes. We also wanted to do this in a manner that the students would enjoy. The students' first assignment was to write autobiographies describing themselves and their families. Then they sought additional information about their heritage from other family members. They were encouraged to interview family members and to ask their subjects to tell them stories about the earlier years. Everyone enjoys listening to a good story. When possible, they recorded the voices for future use. They took photographs and short videos using the school cameras and scanned vintage photographs to add to their research.

They brought all of their material back to the classroom and created storyboards. The students decided which written work, pictures, and voices to add to each page. After all of the material had been sorted into a timeline, they used Microsoft PowerPoint to create slides of their materials. Once the slides were done, the voices were added to the visuals. Books, CDs, videos, and Internet research were used to enrich the learning experience. Using microphones, photographs, and recorded voices to narrate the work, all completed assignments were saved to a CD and presented to the class. As a culminating event, artwork was displayed, and selected students presented their multimedia presentations at a PTSA meeting.

Each activity for this unit was chosen to create an interest and to persuade the students to further explore other cultures. The presentation is designed to encourage the students to explore their own heritage more deeply and to become more familiar with their past. To increase student understanding of diverse cultures, we sought to provide an artistic, technology-assisted, multicultural unit of study through which students would discover that all cultural groups have made significant contributions to civilization and would gain insight into their own lives and the lives of others.

Goals and Objectives

Goal: The main goal of "Exploring Diversity Through Technology" is to assist students as they develop a respect and appreciation for cultural diversity.

Objectives: Students will demonstrate

1. An understanding of culture-related artwork for each culture of study

2. That through research and observation, a self-narrated multi-media presentation can be achieved

▨ Benefits to Students

By the end of this unit, the students were

- Able to effectively operate a digital camera, recorder, and headset microphone
- Able to use PowerPoint to create a dynamic multimedia presentation
- Able to burn their work to a CD-R
- Prepared for evaluation by fellow students

As students investigate historical context and purpose for art and the study of history from various geographic locations, they will gain insight into the lives of others. They will also become increasingly able to reflect upon and respect the origins of their own culture and that of others. If students learn to appreciate and respect one another, parents, teachers, and the community will benefit by experiencing a decrease in violence against people who are from another ethnicity. The long-term goal is a safer school and safer community.

▨ Evaluation Evidence

Objective 1

1. **Baseline data** will be obtained from a pretest administered at the beginning of the semester. Students will create a project reflecting their knowledge and understanding of that culture.

2. **Interim data** will be rubric assessed to determine students' development of the project.

3. **Summative data** will be determined by information received from a posttest at the end of the unit period. The teacher and the students will prepare the artworks and presentations to host a PTSA "Diversity and Technology Night," inviting members of the community to share our classroom experiences.

Objective 2

1. **Baseline data** will be collected using a checklist to determine the students' knowledge and readiness for Internet research and observation culminating in a self-narrated multimedia presentation that will be shown with the art pieces.

2. **Interim data** will be assessed using a six-point rubric for writing.

3. **Summative data** collected from the unit will be interpreted to formulate conclusions and design future study. These data will also prove whether the project was successful.

Curriculum Standards for Visual Art

To implement a multicultural program that includes investigation of various cultures and related artworks, the following visual arts standards will be used:

1.b. Students will select and apply the most effective media, techniques, and processes to communicate their experiences and ideas through their artworks.

1.c. Students will use art materials and tools in a safe and responsible manner.

5.c. Students will analyze, interpret, and evaluate their visual preferences in their own artworks, in nature, and in artworks from various cultures and historical periods.

3.b. Students will evaluate how particular choices of subject matter, symbols, and ideas function to communicate meaning in their own artworks and those of others.

◼ Curriculum Standards for Social Studies

8.1.1. Discuss the nature, challenges, and contributions of African American and/or Native American culture; women and their role in society; and other ethnic and religious groups.

Identify cultural expressions of life in South Carolina and the United States during this period.

8.6.2. Identify and explain historical, geographic, social, and economic factors that have helped shape American democracy.

Helpful Tips

- Make sure all equipment is cataloged and numbered.
- All students should check out and sign off on each item they take out.
- Give each student a time limit on equipment so that it is available for the next student. (Some students will keep them indefinitely if you let them.)
- Give students planning sheets for their presentation so that when they get to the computer, no time is wasted.
- Assign computer time to each student.

My students thoroughly enjoyed this experience. They learned so much more about their heritage than they thought they would and loved being trusted with the equipment. They learned about deadlines and responsibility and did a good job with both.

CHAPTER 10

When They "Just Don't Get It"

Homework and Study Skills

Monique Wallen

Sunrise, Florida

F or many students, social studies is akin to learning a foreign language. They often utter, "I just don't get it." "I hate social studies!" "Social studies is boring!" "I'm no good at social studies!" My students were no exception. How could I change their perceptions? I needed answers. It was time for a change. My students read from the textbook and other sources; participated in many hands-on and fun activities; wrote and acted out plays; went on Internet scavenger hunts; created dioramas; made mobiles; and designed paper plate replicas of major social studies concepts, events, and people. Why did they bomb

This is dedicated to the greatest teacher of all teachers.

their tests? We had done the hands-on "thing" in addition to using the textbook! Students were actively engaged! I asked students what happened and would get responses like "I studied!" "I knew the answers but didn't know how to explain it!" and "I didn't get it!"

When I questioned them further by asking them how much they studied, how they actually studied, and why they couldn't explain the answers, the truth came to light. The students time and time again told me they had studied by looking over the pages a few times. They told me that they "studied" (crammed) the night before the test. Some students said they just didn't "get" what they were reading. Some said they started to fall asleep after rereading the first paragraph. No wonder they couldn't explain a topic in depth. No wonder some barely passed or even failed their tests. Explicit study skills and strategies for tackling nonfiction reading were the missing pieces to the puzzle.

I had some trepidation when it came to the introduction of a study skills program in the classroom. I purposely did not venture into this area because of several painful encounters. I had just switched schools, exchanging one set of clientele for another. At my former school, parents expected and encouraged teachers to include study skills in their lessons. At my new school, the views were quite the opposite. I discovered this after I sent home a packet that included study tips encouraging students to study in a quiet, well-lit area. Parents were asked to check over their student's work before the student turned it in the next day. I thought the packet would be an aid to parents, not a detriment.

Parents subsequently wrote and called in to tell me that they didn't agree with the homework tips. They felt it was their choice how their child studied. The lesson here is to always know the customer or client. I now realize this new set of clientele didn't want any tips or help on the home front, any help was viewed as intrusive. I found the courage to implement an optional study skills program. If parents did not want their children to learn study skills, they could opt out. After implementing a study skills program and teaching strategies for tackling nonfiction reading, I began to see major improvements in test scores and overall performance levels.

Helpful Tips

- Always know your customer or client.
- Send home a weekly information sheet that updates students and parents on upcoming units and tests. The weekly information sheet that I send home is called the "Classroom Scoop." It has pictures of ice cream cones on it along with a box for a parental signature. The parental signature ensures they have seen the upcoming units and tests for the week.
- Teach students how to take notes. It doesn't have to be boring. Students can write their notes in a variety of student-made mini-books that incorporate important concepts.
- Begin and end each day with a review of the previous lessons. This could involve a mini-quiz, a "yesterday I learned" postcard, or a "ticket out the door" or "sum it up" pass.
- Consider incorporating historical fiction novels into social studies. For example, my students read *The Witch of Blackbird Pond* by Elizabeth George Speare during a study of colonial America.
- Create a study guide for upcoming tests. To help students focus on the most important concepts, my study guides only cover what will be on their test.
- Teach students how to find the main idea of a selection. Many of my students have a hard time whittling down information into a concise summary. We often practice for months before they are able to successfully master this skill. My beginning lesson involves reading *The True Story of the Three Little Pigs* by Jon Scieszka. Next I have students pinpoint eight major events of this story. Students have a hard time deciding what constitutes a major event, and thus a mini-lesson will ensue. Last, students have to whittle the eight main events down to a ten-word summary of the main crux of the book. I tell students that each word is worth a dime and that their goal is to have a $1.00 summary. This is one of the most important lessons for my students because when reading nonfiction in particular, they will have to constantly break down material read into smaller, manageable chunks and commit those main ideas to memory.

- Teach students how to become excellent listeners, and how to know when their mind is wandering, and how to get back on track.
- Teach students how to skim text for important details.
- Teach students the variety of ways that index cards can be used. For example, students can use the cards to play Concentration or to create question-and-answer note cards or picture clue note cards.
- Play Jeopardy in the classroom as a review of previously taught topics.
- Teach students how to selectively underline or highlight text as an aid in pinpointing main concepts or events.
- Have students create practice tests with an answer key so they can test themselves or others. Collect these student-created tests and use some of the questions on your classroom test.
- Have students create picture dictionaries for vocabulary terms from their social studies textbook.
- Have students create mnemonics for key terminology.
- Encourage students to find a study buddy. Many students enjoy working with a classmate to review material. Also, remind students that a friend may not be an ideal study buddy since there could be an irresistible urge to talk about unrelated topics.
- Have students complete a weekly self-evaluation. After setting goals, students are to evaluate how close they came to reaching those goals. Save these self-evaluations for use in future parent, student, and teacher conferences.
- Try to incorporate projects that encourage community and parental involvement. For example, every year as a part of an immigration unit, parents and various community members are invited into our classroom for "A Taste of the Nations." On this day, students learn from guest chefs and speakers, essays, scrapbooks, poetry, dance, and music. Students chronicle the history of their family's journey to America. Broward County, Florida, is composed of a diverse population, and this project boosts students' self-esteem and self-worth in a positive way by affirming their uniqueness.

■ Try to incorporate other disciplines into your social studies units. For example, in the unit "Seeking Shelter: From Domes to Skyscrapers," students study how architecture has evolved over time, architectural wonders of the world, and famous architects and scientists. Students create replicas of Frank Lloyd Wright's stained glass windows while exploring mathematical concepts like two-dimensional and three-dimensional shapes, area, and perimeter. Students read about William Jenney's skyscrapers and try to recreate skyscrapers out of toothpicks. Students study matter, atoms, and elements. They recreate Buckminster Fuller's geodesic dome. A culminating activity involves students researching other famous architects and scientists and then making presentations.

PART II

High School

CHAPTER 11

Putting the "Social" Back Into Social Studies

Megan E. Garnett

Fairfax, Virginia

T hree years ago, a student groaned, "Miss Garnett, just tell us what you want us to know! I don't see why you tell us all these stories when they aren't going to be on the test." He used the word "stories" with such disdain that I paused. Troubled by his comment, I calmly explained that teachers use "stories" to make learning meaningful and to help them connect with the past. My response placated my student at the time, but his initial comment continued to haunt me. I wondered if students thought everything that "won't be on a test" was meaningless.

My goal each school year is to share the quirky, fun, heart-wrenching, and even depressing stories of the people and events of America's past. There is an additional common element. Most of my stories involve social experiences. While not all of the stories students hear in their social studies classes are considered "essential knowledge" on our state exam, anecdotal stories help students appreciate history, help students link history to their own experiences, and ultimately lead them to seek more knowledge.

History is more meaningful when we look at the people who shaped the past as social creatures. I don't want my students memorizing dates and facts. I want them to dig deep into history, experience it, and enjoy it. Recent trends in social studies education emphasize the need to personalize history for students. I want students to see themselves in history and think of history as a fun course of study.

Periodically, I devote one 90-minute class period to celebrate an individual, a group of people, an event, or a concept in history. It all started with a lesson on the Great Awakening. After delivering Jonathan Edwards's sermon "Sinners in the Hands of an Angry God," we discussed the characteristics of this period of religious revival. At some point, we went on a tangent and began talking about Halloween and the role religion played in its development. As a result of that informal discussion, I decided that on the 31st of October we would examine the history of Halloween and share historical ghost stories. No social event is complete without snacks, so armed with doughnuts, apple cider, and candy corn, I arrived at school ready to share the fruits of my research.

I pushed aside all of the desks in my room, drew the blinds, and set up the food. Students were told to grab some food and find a place to lounge on the floor. Once everyone was comfortable, I grabbed my flashlight and a stack of ghost stories, and turned off the lights. My intent was to simulate a campfire reading of ghost stories, while relating what we were doing to history. The History Channel's Web site was a valuable resource for the history of Halloween. A local magazine had published ghost stories involving local points of interest, and the bookstore had a great collection of ghost stories, including a number that discussed hauntings in the White House. After each story, we shared our perceptions about ghosts and our experiences. Students got into the activity and shared ghost stories they had heard. No standardized test was going to ask my students about the history of Halloween or who haunts the White House, but they learned that day that history can be fun and interesting.

This Halloween activity inspired me to develop additional activities to make history more meaningful without detracting from the content I am required to teach. While I did all of the work on the Halloween activity, it motivated me to put my students in charge. My subsequent activities have required students to conduct research, reflect on historical issues, and delve into their personal histories. Each lesson involves some research, a writing component, and an artistic feature, in addition to an oral presentation. To add to the social experience, we generally have food. These activities enable my students to relate to history and see it through a different lens. Students demonstrate their critical thinking skills and creativity. Although these lessons aren't explicitly emphasized in the district social studies standards, I am confident that they are worthwhile. Students use critical thinking skills, express themselves creatively, and gain experience in public speaking. I want my students to embrace history and recognize that learning can be a fun and a collaborative effort.

I have developed the following lessons:

Presidential Retirement Gala. At the end of the year, a fellow English teacher asks her students to bring in food dishes that are symbolic representations of literature they have read over the course of the year. I have adapted her idea in many ways for my history classes, and one of my favorites is the celebration of the presidential administrations of our first four presidents.

Students are assigned to one of four groups: Washington, Adams, Jefferson, and Madison. Students are required to write a retirement speech as though they are their assigned president. Using Washington's Farewell Address as an example, students must highlight the achievements of their assigned presidential administration and offer advice to the nation and future presidents. Within each group, students pair off and develop a food dish that celebrates an achievement or highlights a controversy. Finally, each pair must develop a "playlist" and bring in three songs from any era to play at the party. These songs must symbolize their assigned president. In this lesson, students collaborate on different levels and use their critical thinking skills. Groups choose the best speech to deliver at the party. Each pair explains their song selections while they play in the background.

Happy 300th Birthday, Ben Franklin! On January 17, 2006, we commemorated Benjamin Franklin's 300th birthday. I unveiled the idea two weeks before, and months earlier we learned about Franklin's contributions to American history. I asked students to recall what they remembered of Franklin. We determined that he was a true Renaissance man and was remembered not only for his intelligence, but for his quirkiness.

Students could choose from one of three poster projects. Choices included illustrating a "Franklinism" by explaining one of Franklin's many adages (for example, a penny saved is a penny earned), celebrating one of his inventions, or developing a "Franklin the _____" poster characterizing Franklin based on biographical research. Examples of student characterizations included Franklin the diplomat, the inventor, the weatherman, the ladies' man, and the writer. I provided secondary sources to assist students with their research. These included *Poor Richard's Almanac*, Lincoln's autobiography, and Web sites. No birthday party is complete without a birthday cake, so I brought in a cake for each class. As students enjoyed their cake, they listened to their peers present their posters to the class. Students were surprised to learn how many inventions and adages Franklin contributed.

Funerals as a Social Experience. Birthdays are not the only way to remember an important figure in history; funerals are also effective. I have students write obituaries of historical figures, highlighting their achievements. This is a good way to review and to start students' writing. After discussing the format and style of writing an obituary, I put the lights on low; play soft, yet moving music (Enya works well); and prepare the kids to write. We have even noted the deaths of time periods and empires. We wrote an obituary for the end of Spanish colonial rule in South America.

What Does It Mean to Be Free? This is a great question to pose to students as an introduction to the Civil Rights Movement; it fosters reflection and helps them personalize the concept of freedom. I teach the Civil Rights Movement after Reconstruction so my students can follow the plight of African Americans from the passage of the 13th Amendment to the passage of the Civil Rights Acts of 1964 and 1968. I ask students to think about how the slaves felt about the passage of the 13th Amendment and the subsequent "Civil War amend-ments" (14th and 15th). What do you think the slaves expected? How do you think freedom felt when the Supreme Court handed down the *Plessy v. Ferguson* (1896) decision?

I keep the assignment's criteria purposely vague to inspire student creativity. Students answer the question of what it means to be free with a collage of pictures and/or words, a poem, an essay, or a song. One year, a student even created a sculpture. All students present their "answers" to the class. This is one of the most powerful days of the school year.

Women's History Tea Party. I developed this idea with a friend and colleague as a way to celebrate Women's History Month. Students are assigned to research the achievements and biography of an influential woman. They present their historical figure's history in a structured essay titled "Personality Portrait." They decorate a cookie or make a "tea sandwich" based on the personality of the woman they researched. On the day of the celebration, students bring in their portraits and their food selection. I provide tea and lemonade. The portraits are posted around the room in gallery fashion and students enjoy their beverages, cookies, and sandwiches as they peruse the portraits. I encourage students to spend time with an influential woman in their lives.

Historical Road Trip. I put students in cooperative learning groups and ask them to create a passenger list for a bus trip across the United States. They have to include themselves and ten figures from U.S. history. Then they explain the rationale for their choices.

As they present their lists, it is clear that they have learned a good deal about many historical figures over the course of the school year. Most students include John D. Rockefeller on their list because they want to "travel in luxury!" One year, a group assigned seats to their passengers. This group chose Ben Franklin and Martin Luther King, Jr. They put Martin Luther King, Jr., in the driver's seat of the bus because "He will never have to sit in the back of the bus again!" I told them about Franklin's penchant for taking "air baths," so they put Ben Franklin on top of the bus because "No naked people were allowed in the bus." This activity sparked many fun discussions.

I decided to add a geography component to this lesson. I formed groups of four and asked them to put together a cross-country vacation including ten figures from history. Each group was required to choose people from at least four different time periods. They drew maps on heavy poster board and developed an itinerary with fourteen stops (one for each student and one for each historical figure). The stops had to be significant to the historical figure and could not be their homes. We used Neil Armstrong as an example. We thought the first man to walk on the moon would like to visit Roanoke, Virginia, the site of the "Lost Colony" and the first place the English settled in North America. In addition to the passenger list, the map, and the itinerary, students had to create a list of at least ten "must-have" items they needed to take on the bus. They had to explain how these items would be useful to the entire group. The "Road Trips" were presented on the last day of class as a review of the school year.

Sports Challenge. This is an assignment for extra credit when we discuss the California Gold Rush. Students inevitably experience an "ah-ha" moment when they realize the San Francisco 49ers football team was named in honor of the speculators who "rushed" to California in search of gold in 1849. I remind them that history is everywhere, and then I encourage them to sift through the names of professional sports teams to find references from historical events, peoples, and terms. They must bring in a list and an explanation of how the team name or mascot is historically significant.

Helpful Tips

- Some of these activities require a financial and time commitment (in terms of both planning and classroom time), so start off by trying one each grading period. Also consider contacting your PTO to get help with funds if necessary.
- Be flexible. Keeping a good pace to prepare for standardized testing is important, but the time devoted to these types of activities does reinforce learning and engage students on different levels.
- Ask your students for ideas or suggestions to modify the activities. One year, my students asked to create models of the key battles of the Civil War, so we turned the classroom into a mini-museum.

CHAPTER *12*

A Social Studies Twist on the "Hemingway Challenge"

Megan E. Garnett

Fairfax, Virginia

L ast school year, I picked up an old copy of *Utne*, a quirky magazine a professor recommended. The magazine is a collection of
articles found in other publications. I was inspired by an interesting
piece called "The Hemingway Challenge" in *BlackBook* magazine.
Ernest Hemingway, a great American writer, was once asked if he
could write a six-word novel. He wrote, "For Sale. Baby shoes. Never
used." I thought this challenge could be adapted for my class and my
students could write six-word novels. The six-word submissions were
fascinating and quite funny, although not all were appropriate to share
with my students. I decided to modify this six-word novel idea for
students to review the key laws in a unit on the Reconstruction.

My student teacher and I developed samples for the kids, and they had difficulty. It didn't take long to realize that six words were just not enough, so we changed the rule to ten words. We developed our samples, and the extra word allowance made this much easier. After writing two novels of ten words, we studied them to see if they could be shortened to six words, but it was impossible. We decided a ten-word limit was more reasonable. The next day, we were excited to present our challenge to the students.

After recounting the story of Hemingway's challenge and sharing his "novel," we discussed whether they could write a story with six words. Their responses were mixed, but generally positive. In groups of two or three, the students were asked to choose one key Reconstruction law and develop a definition and explanation of the effects of the law in ten words. Once the students determined their ten-word descriptor, they wrote it on large sheets of butcher paper. Each group challenged the entire class to figure out which law they were describing. I hoped this activity would prove to be a good review lesson and a fun way to study these laws. The kids worked diligently debating word choice, focusing on the most important aspects of their assigned law, and noting contextual clues. I was impressed with the final results. My student teacher and I decided to create a PowerPoint presentation with each group's final ten-word descriptor, and we used it in other classes as a way to review the Reconstruction.

This year, I pulled the PowerPoint presentation out again and shared it with my new group of students. As a class, we debated what the previous class was thinking and what law they were describing. There were a number of times the students could narrow the descriptor down to a couple of laws and then zero in. We were finally able to decipher which law was represented. This resulted in a great activity to reinforce the importance of taking the time to read slowly and carefully, focusing on the contextual clues. In addition, both last year's students and this year's students worked well as a group as they talked through the development of their descriptors.

They debated the meanings of the descriptors. This dialogue was important in reinforcing student learning and enhancing students' comprehension. Students this year were then challenged to create as many new descriptors as they could, using last year's challenge as a model. I had fun developing samples for this activity and then working with the small groups as they tackled this challenge. Teachers are often thinking about new ideas and methods for teaching their students, and I have found inspiration in a variety of places. While not all of my new ideas are as successful as I'd like them to be, *BlackBook* via *Utne* provided a great and fun challenge.

Teacher samples:

1. New owners, ½ million strong; 160 acres plowed, 5-year commitment. (Homestead Act)

2. Election politics end Reconstruction. Whites win, do blacks? (Compromise of 1877)

Student samples:

1. States ratify, whites peeved. Blacks freed, but still in need. (13th Amendment)

2. Equally protected despite race, color, or servitude; whites angry. (14th Amendment)

3. Races neutralized; check the boxes; beware of snowstorm. (15th Amendment)

4. Preview to 14th Amendment—citizenship, equal protection; whites say, "seriously?" (Civil Rights Act of 1866)

5. Assisting refugees, ex-slaves; veto overridden. Hallelujah! (Freedmen's Bureau Act)

6. Voting watched, troops in place; disguises illegal in every state. (KKK Act)

Helpful Tips

- Take the time to share Hemingway's six-word novel and discuss students' interpretations of the novel.
- Providing examples for students is critical to help them understand the activity.
- Have students use highlighters to underscore context clues in their vocabulary definitions before starting the challenge.

CHAPTER 13

World War II Memories

An Oral History Project

Marguerite Ames

Norwich, Vermont

This intergenerational project inspires students to preserve and value American history by giving them the opportunity to actively participate in the documenting process. After or during their study of World War II, students, individually or in small groups, interview a World War II veteran or a civilian who lived through that period. The student focuses on this individual's life just before, during, and after the war to illustrate the changes brought about by the war. Based on these interviews of friends, family members, and neighbors whose lives were touched by World War II, the essays provide snapshots of life in the early 1940s. Beyond the interviews and essays, students illustrate their work, which is displayed at school. Ultimately, their work can be assembled into a book; we sold copies to underwrite professional printing costs, but you could also assemble the work using desktop publishing tools.

Another possibility, with the support of your local historical society or library, is to find World War II artifacts to display, including uniforms and equipment, scrapbooks, photographs, military medals, and letters or journals. Community members will be happy to contribute memorabilia from late relatives. This exhibit brings exposure to the project and creates an interest in the period. We opened the exhibit during a book reception for the students, their families, and the veterans. We held it on the lawn of the town historical society.

In addition to exposing students to the diversity of human experience during World War II, the project offers something equally valuable: a direct link to a past rapidly disappearing from living memory. Without exception, my students learned that individuals carry a past that can be neither gleaned at first glance nor truly imagined. The hope is that projects such as this will pass down memories from one generation to another. This will help ensure that events of the past will remain a vital part of the collective consciousness of our generation and future generations.

This document reflects my experiences and my personal vision for the oral history project. However, the project could also center around a different event, and the possibilities within living memory are legion: a more recent armed conflict, a natural disaster, a civil rights demonstration, an assassination, the first NASA moon landing, and so forth. It is up to you to make this project your own!

▨ Getting Started: Resources

Administration

Ultimately you'll need substantial support—scheduling, monetary, PR—from the principal, the superintendent, or both. Describe the project in sufficient detail to the administration. As the project proceeds, keep them updated, especially with the schedule to avoid conflicts. Be sure to secure a commitment to fund layout and printing. There is an up-front cost that has to be paid, although in the long run this could be a fundraiser, if the resulting book is sold.

Teacher/Coordinator (You!)

The coordinator teaches the students how to conduct interviews, takes notes, write essays, and improve and polish their writing. Someone has to take responsibility for the overall planning. This includes recruiting the interview subjects, coordinating a schedule, assembling the essays into electronic versions, and working with a printer. Although I was ultimately responsible for all of this, I delegated some tasks, or components of those tasks, to my student teacher and a part-time classroom assistant. Find one or a few parents to assume the roles of editor and layout specialist. I found parents to work on the layout and final editing of the book and to help with the design of the cover.

Support from families and colleagues is essential. Parents are needed to drive students to and from interviews. They also supervise the interviews and help students with notes and follow-up questions. Some parents typed while others organized the book reception, which we held on the lawn of the historical society. If this is a team effort, you will need a strong commitment from the other teachers involved and a clear division of labor. When the presentation date approaches, you may want student art, decorations, and a musical presentation (our school band played "Boogie Woogie Bugle Boy" as a signal for everyone to take their seats).

▧ Interview Subjects

At the beginning of the project, you will need to focus on finding and communicating with the interview subjects. Initial contact should be by phone, but many letters should be sent to thank them for agreeing to participate. The letters should include interview instructions, a copy of the student biography so they can change factual errors if necessary, and an invitation to the dedication. Be sure to include a self-addressed stamped envelope to make it easier for them to respond.

You need at least one subject for every three students. A town chapter of the American Legion helped us find subjects, and we also used word of mouth. Since this is a rapidly disappearing population, we cast our net out further. To make a clear connection with local history, we interviewed many individuals who lived in our town during the war years but did not serve in the war. In addition to achieving a more global perspective, we encouraged students to interview relatives and friends who lived through the war years but, aside from the students, had no connections to the town. Students who conducted these "personal" interviews worked alone, while those with the other interview subjects worked in groups of two or three. Once you recruit enough subjects, prepare a spreadsheet with the names, addresses, and phone numbers of the subjects. It's helpful to make a spreadsheet listing student names, their assigned subjects, the date and location of their interview, and the supervising adult. This will probably need to be updated often.

In addition to human resources, you will need equipment:

Digital cameras—for candid shots during the interviews. These photos must be taken at high resolution, and the resolution must be consistent.

Graphics scanner—for old photos and other memorabilia. You may want to include some of theses images in the book. They must be scanned at no less than 300 dpi. You need a good scanner and the technical skills to make sure the resolution is correct. It takes quite a while to scan properly, so photos will have to be left for one week and retrieved/returned later. Make sure to record data on everything that you scan, including names of people and objects in the picture and the location—information you may want for the captions. (Adults took some photos for the book during the interviews. We tried to get period photos of the subjects. We included some recent images, but the vintage photos definitely contributed to the feeling of the book.)

Tape recorders and tapes—for more accurate notes. Students simply cannot take notes fast enough to keep up with the interviews. So, each group needs a tape recorder and tapes for all the sessions. I suggest that the tapes be pre-labeled (who's being interviewed, date, subject). If possible, use a fresh tape for each interview, rather than reusing the tapes. Students will transcribe the interviews later.

Computers—for authors to write their essays. If you choose to publish the interviews in a book, the files will ultimately be collected and submitted to the person or company (publisher) that will do the layout for the book.

▧ Preparing for the Interviews

1. Practice questions: I had students interview my student teacher about what she did during the summer. I divided the class into three groups, by table. One table was responsible for questions leading up to the event, one table was in charge of questions about the event, and the third table asked questions about the event's aftermath. Each student had to ask a question, recording both the question and the response. Then we discussed which question elicited the most information, and came up with guidelines about preparing interview questions and how the students could improve their original questions. Students asked some of the improved questions to see if the improvements worked. (45 to 60 minutes)

2. Mock interviews: Pairs of students interviewed each other. First, students elicited a general topic from their partner about something they did over the summer. Then, the students wrote questions for the interview. They took turns interviewing each other. During the interview, the subjects were instructed to respond only to the question asked. Finally, they wrote compositions based on the information obtained through the interview. They read their compositions aloud to each other. Subsequent discussion included the very important idea of follow-up questions. (two 45- to 60-minute class periods)

3. Data sheets: After individuals agreed to participate in the interview, we sent them forms to fill out and return to us before the interview, so the students could digest them. These provided students with some context for the interview. Most looked them over just before the interview due to time constraints.

4. Interview questions: After discussing the differences of subjects, we prepared two sets of questions: one for military personnel and one for civilians. Each class divided into two groups (military and civilian), which, in turn, divided into three

subgroups responsible for questions focusing on before, during, and after the war. The next day, groups read all of the questions from both classes and selected those they thought would result in the best interview. Some of the questions were combined and edited. I took the liberty of clarifying and expanding some questions for the final interview worksheets. Also, I attempted to put them in a reasonable order, in terms of flow. (two 45- to 60-minute class periods)

5. Interview etiquette and follow-up questions: My student teacher and I did a brief mock interview as an example to show students what not to do: my student teacher didn't shake hands or make eye contact, interrupted, scratched and yawned, slouched, and tapped her feet. Students came up with a list of etiquette expectations. This list was given to all interview supervisors to review before the interview with their groups. We also discussed follow-up questions again. (one 45- to 60-minute class period)

▧   From Interview to Essay

Conducting the Interviews

We conducted the interviews over several days. A few of the subjects came to the school, but given their ages, we decided to go to them. Many were in assisted-living facilities, so parents took their groups to their homes for interviews. For interviews done in school, we used the library as well as the classroom, to assure privacy and relative quiet. A few subjects chose to be interviewed at the local historical society. Students doing "personal" interviews (family, for example) did these on their own time as homework.

Ideally, one parent volunteer should be assigned to every group. The volunteer should go over etiquette, make sure the interviews run smoothly. The parent should help the students stay on topic and manage the tape recorders. I encourage these supervisors to interject follow-up questions, if the student agrees. Some volunteers take notes, as well, which is a very good idea to help with factual accuracy!

Because students did not all interview at the same time, I assigned reading and map work for all students to do independently. In addition, when they were finished interviewing, students could listen to the tapes and fix, clarify, and enhance their notes. Students requiring certain educational accommodations worked one-on-one with adults.

Writing the Essays

1. Before the students wrote their essays, I wrote my expectations. After the students annotated their notes to suggest an outline, they started writing. Before conferencing with a teacher, students had to self-edit for "responsibilities" and peer-edit.

2. While waiting for conferences, students worked on illustrations, poems, collages, and so forth.

3. After students made revisions based on feedback from the first conference, they had second conferences to work on the finer points. Only after the second conference could students type their essays on the computer.

4. Most students (and some parents) typed the essays at home, as the final step in the writing process. I asked parents to work with the students to proofread the final drafts.

Book Preparation (Optional)

Validation—Send a copy of the "final draft" of each essay to the subject of the interview with a request for factual corrections. In many cases, the students misunderstood their notes or the tape and wrote something incorrectly. Having the vets make factual corrections was invaluable. It also showed them that we were making progress.

Assemble book—Each section or chapter of the book should be in its own word processing file, created in a program such as Microsoft Word. Make sure you use the program and format specified by whoever is doing the layout. It will be better, especially if someone is volunteering his or her time! In our case, the foreword, each chapter, and the acknowledgments were all separate files. In fact, we made a separate directory for each individual and added text, scanned photos, and other items in their directory so it was well organized for the layout task.

Edit book—Go through each student file and do a spelling and grammar check before sending the files to the layout specialist.

Write foreword or introduction—Have someone else edit it!

Submit text, graphics, and cover for layout—This can be done on a CD, or by e-mail if everyone has high-speed Internet connections. Also include all scanned graphics on the CD. Make sure that they are clearly labeled with names and captions. We also divided our book into sections (At the Homefront, In the Service, Around the World) and included a table of contents.

Proof the book—After the layout, you'll get a bunch of files back, most likely as many as you submitted. It probably won't be possible for you to edit them directly. Print a copy of the "book" and find the errors—they're there, just keep looking, or have an independent party look. Also look for formatting and layout inconsistencies and errors. Do all of the chapters look alike? Is pagination where you want it? Do essays always start on a right-hand page? We decided to use pull quotes as well as photos to create harmonious spreads. In addition, we had a parent create collages for section divisions. I selected quotations that I hoped were meaningful for each division spread.

Proof the layout—After corrections, repeat the above procedures twice more. Use a different editor each time, if possible.

Submit corrections (layout, text errors)

Proof second layout, submit corrections (text errors)

Proof third layout, submit corrections—Especially recheck all name attributions for photo captions. Remember, any errors sent to the printer cost money to be fixed!

Send final layout to printer—Depending on the printer, they may send you a final galley to proof again. From that point, it will probably take a few weeks.

▨ Calendar (Ours)

Spring/early September: Determine whether there are other interested teachers. Obtain commitment of support (financial and spiritual) from the administration. If you want to do an exhibit at your local historical society, contact them now!

Early September: Ask for parent volunteers for supervising interviews, editing student work, and helping with the reception. Identify, contact, and write to potential interview subjects. Ask families if they have a friend or relative their child could interview. It wouldn't hurt to have an extra one or two in case some subjects have to pull out of the project. When talking to interview subjects, determine their availability for interviews. Ideally, you want to do all of the interviews on the same day. We were unable to do this, so we scheduled them over the course of a week.

Late September: Schedule volunteers to supervise the interviews. Gather necessary equipment. Send the subjects a letter confirming the time, date, and location of the interview, and explain it in detail. Include the data sheet or questionnaire; a pre-addressed, stamped return envelope; and the due date. Follow up by phone to answer any questions.

Early October: Teach interview skills. Confirm each interview appointment with the subject the day before it is to take place.

Mid-October: Teach World War II background. Complete the interviews.

Mid- to late-October: Write and edit the essays.

If you wish to publish a book of the interviews and essays:

November: Copy all of the essays, graphics, and pictures onto a single CD.

January: Write and edit the introduction, foreword, and other text. Prepare the initial CD, organized by essay for the editor or layout specialist.

February: Send the CD to the editor or layout specialist. Get a printing cost estimate based on the size of the book. Get a final commitment from the superintendent to pay for printing costs.

March: Do three iterations of editing the layout and sending corrections and changes to the publisher.

April: Turn the project output over to the printer.

If you wish to hold a publication event:

Early May: Start planning the book presentation or reception. This is the time to contact the press about the event. Send the announcement home with students. Mobilize parent volunteers. Send formal invitations to interview subjects and other guests. Follow up with calls and arrange transportation if necessary. Hope that the books arrive soon!

Late May: Confirm all plans. Enjoy the reception!

CHAPTER 14

Life-Changing Field Trips

James Wade D'Acosta

Fairfield, Connecticut

L ife-changing field trips consume 30 hours of intricate planning. Pulling students out of other classes inconveniences colleagues, and standardized testing mania increases pressure to keep students in their seats. Furthermore, there are many tempting field trip destinations. Therefore, core principles are essential: Destinations must have an exceptional potential to elicit emotional responses from visitors, multiple resources must be used to advantage during a trip, and students must see that the topics addressed during a trip are valued by adults. Such trips can be short and inexpensive.

Gettysburg

Emotion drives intellect. When students are challenged emotionally, they focus their minds, search for answers, and sometimes make lifelong decisions. I design experiences to build to a crescendo of emotional intensity in order to instill civic dispositions of patriotism, respect for veterans, compassion for adversaries, and tolerance of various religious and cultural traditions. Testimonials by students in reflective essays demonstrate that my finest lessons in class fail to instill these dispositions, but that our field trips are much more memorable. Here's how Kerri put it following our trip to Gettysburg National Military Park:

> Throughout all of elementary, middle, and some of high school, I had been taught about this huge Civil War in America and how it was so important. I basically took the notes, passed the test, and let the American Civil War be gone until the next time I was forced to remember it.
>
> A "real" experience came to me during our trip in the cemetery. Our tour guide brought us to the Connecticut burial plot. "Oh great," I thought, "Mr. D'Acosta probably told this tour guide to show us about our own state. Why do I care? How is this going to help me on the AP test?" Honestly, I ignored every word the tour guide was saying.
>
> As we were leaving the cemetery, I looked once again at all those graves. Right then, I realized that the Civil War was actually a real thing; people did in fact die for this cause. It wasn't just something from out of a textbook.
>
> Not only did this part of the trip make the Civil War more real to me, but it also made me realize that not everything is made just to memorize for a test. Seeing the graves really showed me that this is not all about getting college credit by passing a test for a challenging class. In the long run, my score on the AP test won't even matter. But seeing these graves is an important reminder that will stay with me forever. People died in an effort to make this country the absolutely fabulous one it is today. And now, I really do thank them for that.

Gettysburg has graves, monuments, vistas, and expert interpreters. Gettysburg works while most other battlefields do not. Nonetheless, poor planning can defeat a superstar destination. A winning design might include the following:

- Assigning written work on the causes of the war.
- Giving a brief extra credit assignment of finding a poem, statistic, or story about the war to share with classmates.
- Giving an optional reading assignment, Tony Horwitz's *Confederates in the Attic*, demonstrating that the war affects the behavior of Americans today.
- Watching Ted Turner's *Gettysburg* (based on Michael Shaara's *The Killer Angels*) on the bus ride to Gettysburg, which is 270 miles away.
- Visiting the National Cemetery at Gettysburg, where students can interact with living history actor Jim Getty portraying President Lincoln.
- Taking a five-hour tour of the battlefield led by a licensed battlefield guide, during which the guide includes accounts and monument sites of soldiers from Connecticut: "Connecticut soldiers are buried here; a Connecticut colonel was decapitated there; a 21-year-old Connecticut lieutenant amputated his own shattered leg before slipping into shock and dying over there; be careful not to trip on bones coming up through the topsoil."
- Having students read their extra credit poems, statistics, or stories to the group.
- Having students line up on the mile-wide field of Pickett's Charge. Classmates grip Confederate and Union flags while others sound bugles and drums. Students watch the sun set and listen to classmates perform "Taps."
- Providing students with copies of D. Scott Hartwig's *A Killer Angels Companion* and a selection of other booklets for voluntary future reading.
- During the return trip, watching a movie on Western history, such as *Tombstone*, in which the former standing of characters as Rebels or Yankees is influential.
- Assigning written work on the fighting and aftermath of the war and testing students on this content.
- Making Civil War topics a possible choice for research projects completed during the marking period.
- Encouraging students to teach students at a local elementary school about the war, using their research projects.

This design pulls emotional responses from students within an intellectual framework that helps them understand the Civil War and encourages lifelong dispositions common to outstanding citizens. The progression requires 30 hours of work by the teacher: advanced planning to integrate the field trip into classroom experiences, convincing everyone that the trip is worthwhile, dealing with a bus company, calling Jim Getty, securing a special use permit from the National Parks Service, buying Union and Confederate flags and creating durable flagpoles that can be quickly assembled, ordering *A Killer Angels Companion* and a mix of books to use as prizes, ordering book labels from the graphic arts teacher, collecting permission slips, attracting chaperones, choosing photographs and an essay to submit to the newspaper, and making various gestures to maintain strong working relationships with everyone involved.

Washington, D.C.

Washington is even farther than Gettysburg from my school, but its attractions are irresistible and I go in one long day. The success of these trips in teaching curriculum and impacting students' lives demonstrates that teachers anywhere with access to coach buses and interstate highways can plan life-changing field trips using destinations within a 300-mile radius of their school. The most important factor in running a successful one-day trip to Washington, D.C. is limiting the objectives. I go for the emotional power of the Holocaust Memorial Museum and the Vietnam Memorial Wall.

I time this trip with my lessons on World War II and as a precursor to my lessons on Vietnam. Special details include the following:

- Having a Holocaust survivor speak to students the day before the trip.
- Showing *Life Is Beautiful* and *Schindler's List* during the drive from Fairfield.
- Breaking students into autonomous groups of eight with a single chaperone.
- Requiring each group to view the exhibit on current genocides and pick up fliers that the museum publishes on these events,

which students know relate to an essay due at the end of the marking period proceeding from the thesis statement "I can help prevent genocide by _____, _____, and _____."

- Giving each group three hours of free time after finishing in the Holocaust Memorial Museum.
- Meeting Vietnam combat veterans at the Washington Monument and using them to guide each group through the World War II Memorial, Korean War Memorial, and Vietnam Memorial Wall for about an hour and a half.
- Showing *Full Metal Jacket* and *Good Morning, Vietnam* during the drive home.

Laura's reaction is typical:

The day before we left for Washington, Mr. Walter Feiden, a survivor of Auschwitz, spoke to our class. I learned firsthand how awful the Holocaust was. The Holocaust Memorial Museum however, took that knowledge to a whole new level, one that put images to the facts and made me even sicker with anger. I toured the museum with my two friends, both of whom are Jewish. It was very interesting to me to watch their reactions as they saw what their ancestors had to go through. One thing struck me was when one friend refused to walk through the cattle car that had transported Jews to a concentration camp. For a 16-year-old girl in 2006 to be affected like this shows the continuing horror of the Holocaust.

I run both the Gettysburg and Washington, D.C. trips on Fridays. Each trip costs students about $100 and cash for food and souvenirs. We leave at 5:30 a.m. and return at 11:00 p.m. and 1:00 a.m., respectively, which preserves the weekend.

Closer to Home

Gettysburg and Washington, D.C. are extreme one-day field trips, but potentially life-changing destinations may be just down the block. An eight-hour trip costing students $25 plus cash for lunch takes advantage of local resources but still involves 30 hours of planning. I take students in Highlights of Western Civilization classes and in American History classes to local houses of worship. Ordained clergy lead one-hour discussions in their own sanctuaries: a rabbi, a Catholic or Greek Orthodox priest, a Protestant minister, an Islamic imam, and sometimes a Buddhist monk.

In Highlights of Western Civilization classes, the presentations focus on the beliefs, symbols, and customs making each religion unique and ones it shares with other traditions. For American History classes, the leaders explain the religious motivation of members participating in social activism as displayed throughout our history.

Religion is a controversial topic, but most social studies courses cannot be well taught without its inclusion. Furthermore, students confront religion when their classmates die and when other tragedies occur. Students who participate in religious field trips often get reliable information about religious traditions other than their own for the first time and gain insights that help them cope with difficult and awkward situations throughout their lives, from interfaith marriages to funeral customs to understanding holidays such as Yom Kippur, Easter, and Ramadan.

The day is peppered with profound statements. Therefore, I gather the students together at school before sending them home. Students share their thoughts and reactions and I answer questions. The experience speaks for itself: religion strongly influences our actions; religions share common features and values intended to help people live fulfilling lives; the continued separation of church and state is essential for peace in our society; and the United States maintains a tradition of religious toleration, which we see in our community and in our school.

Most students do not take history courses after high school. If we want them as adults to seek the benefits of visiting historical sites and museums and of speaking to individuals who participated in famous events or who are from different cultures, we should display these life-changing benefits now.

Helpful Tips

Gettysburg

1. Thomas Publications in Gettysburg has a great selection of inexpensive Civil War books, including D. Scott Hartwig's *A Killer Angels Companion*.

Washington, D.C.

1. The Vietnam Veterans Memorial Fund provides the combat veterans who volunteer to walk my students through the recent war memorials.

2. Name the movies you'll show on the bus on the permission slip and include their rating. The ones I show are rated R.

Houses of Worship

1. Visit congregations attended by your students.

2. Consider timing the trip close to Passover and Easter. The rabbi you use may be willing to conduct a model Passover Seder during lunch.

3. Do as much "touch" and "see" as possible. Ask the imam to lead students through a call to prayer, the rabbi to open a Torah scroll, the priest to display the Eucharist, the minister to explain the absence of Jesus from the cross.

4. Publicity takes the issue of tolerance of religious traditions beyond the bounds of the school and into the wider community. This trip is an attractive news item.

CHAPTER 15

Crafting Individualized Research Projects

James Wade D'Acosta

Fairfield, Connecticut

I guide all of my students on research projects every quarter and have done so throughout my career in suburban and urban high schools and middle schools. The procedures I continually refine are the result of teaching American History, Modern World History, Highlights of Western Civilization, Economics, Youth and the Law, and Politics classes. Some students are in classes grouped by ability level; others are not. Research projects and field trips transform students' lives and express my commitment to individualized teaching. My procedures are flexible and successful.

Currently, I teach 120 high school juniors and seniors in five classes of 24 students meeting 44 minutes each day. Research projects account for 20% of quarter grades, the remaining 80% coming from written chapter homework, tests, essays, interviews, and class simulations.

Learning is an inward journey, a process of evolution. It's challenging to guide because some of us learn best through art, music, or literature. Therefore, I use a structure for research projects that opens the curriculum to the personal interests and talents of my students. Students can choose to work alone or with friends, select the topic, and choose how to express their learning: a children's book, model, painting, family scrapbook, persuasive report, video, or reading. I clarify the details on a research contract, which serves as an assessment checklist.

Consider Lisa, who created a portrait of Lincoln during one quarter and a gun control painting in another: "This year I was unable to take an art class in school. Those two projects tapped into my passion and reminded me of the joy I get from creating. Art is also something I hope to pursue for the rest of my life."

Hear Anna: "I have all my lower classman friends confused. They don't know if they should run to get into your class or run to get out because I'm always doing U.S. History homework. This was an awesome year and I'm proud of myself. I went to a Montessori school and I always compare public school to that school. There I was expected to challenge myself and do the best I could, so I did. Your classroom is the closest thing I have found to that style of learning." Students of all ability levels respond with excellence to meaningful opportunities.

Individualized projects capture a student's interest and learning style, but teachers should also push a student into uncomfortable areas. Students resist reading. Remedial students don't read because they're not good at it, and advanced students save time by scanning. Yet writing skills and intellectual life depend on reading experience. Therefore, I require reading projects.

Students may read fiction or nonfiction. Examples in American History include an anthology of Edgar Allan Poe's stories and Tom Brokaw's *The Greatest Generation*. In Economics, students sometimes read Barbara Ehrenreich's *Nickel and Dimed*. Students write journals and a polished paper about the author's expertise, the book's themes, and their personal reflections.

There are six keys to implementing research projects:

- efficiency of class time
- flexibility of topics and modes of expression
- equality of difficulty among research options
- fairness in the effort required and grade awarded
- communication of clear and reliable expectations by the teacher
- immediate application of knowledge gained

Using a syllabus, continually refining templates of various contracts, and distributing exemplary projects help achieve these objectives.

Efficiency: Efficiency looks like chaos at the beginning of each marking period when I pass out a syllabus, describe research options, show examples of projects, and begin meeting individually with students. For four class periods, I meet with students to work out the details of their projects, send others to the library to decide upon or to begin research, and watch others work ahead on other assignments. The project then becomes homework. I note a date for a halfway check on each contract and give students a photocopy.

Flexibility: Empowered people strive for excellence. Our students are not lazy; they're impatient, bored, and unwilling to invest themselves in assignments that remind them of their weaknesses.

Social studies teachers often assess student learning only within a narrow band of skills needed for memorization and analysis expressed through nonfiction writing. Even a casual survey of jobs people hold reveals much more variety. Historical paintings and models require meticulous research, and the completed works express understanding. Writing a children's book requires research, synthesis, and artistic skill.

Equality of difficulty: Students are busy. If one project option is easier than others, students gravitate to it. Trial and error balances the difficulty among project options. For projects requiring 15 hours of work for a grade of B, a student working alone to produce a five-page persuasive research paper with five sources and two posters works as hard as three students producing a 15-minute video with five sources, two students writing a 10-page children's book with five sources, one student creating a painting, a student reading for 12 hours and writing an eight-page journal and a four-page essay, a student building a model, or a student learning two songs.

Fairness: A student devoting 15 hours to an assignment and producing excellent-quality work should receive a substantial grade. If the project counts for less than 20% of a student's quarter grade, it isn't worth the student's effort. If it counts for more, it may squeeze out too many other parts of the curriculum.

Responsibilities are constantly added to our jobs but rarely taken away. Students are similarly overwhelmed by us, their teachers. It is not reasonable to simply add a research project to an existing list of assignments. If projects require 15 hours of work, then 15 hours of other work should be eliminated. Choices have to be made.

In my year-long American History classes, in which the curriculum stretches from the Colonial Period past the Civil Rights Era, students complete detailed written work on five chapters each quarter. I only do detailed class coverage of 20 of the 36 chapters in our textbook. Deciding which chapters best fulfill the curriculum is excruciating.

Communication of clear and reliable expectations: A project worth 20% of a student's grade is decisive to his or her morale. Expectations must be clear and reliable. Research contracts meet these demands beautifully. I finalize my expectations by hand on prepared templates when I meet individually with students. We both sign the contract, which states that meeting the minimum expectations on time and in good quality will yield a grade of B, with an A reserved for greater effort and quality. To earn an A, students may use more sources, write more pages, learn more songs, read for more hours, or teach elementary school children.

I complete the contracts four weeks before the projects are due, give a photocopy to each student, and give a copy to the student's resource teacher if warranted. Two weeks before the projects are due, I note each student's progress and any negotiated changes. When students submit projects, they complete a self-evaluation section, and I write my grading notes in a section reserved for that purpose. I take responsibility for oversights and revise my templates.

For example, my earliest template for a model project did not specify the skill level for a model built from a kit. A student submitted a snap-together model along with the other expectations on the contract: a two-page report with citations and a poster. I awarded a B and improved my template.

These procedures produce high morale and agreement on grades because strong morale depends on communication, fairness, and flexibility. Every year, I have a few students who do little chapter homework, test poorly, and read and write pathetically but excel on creative research projects. Shane was one such student. He passed the two quarters by building models (one was a full-scale model of a Revolutionary War cannon), put forth a Herculean effort on the final exam, and secured a "D for diploma" for the year. Shane's phenomenal models earned him respect and self-esteem.

Immediate application: Students should immediately apply their learning by at least presenting their projects to their classmates. Short presentations force students to synthesize information, and peer pressure encourages them to produce high-quality work.

Students organize their thoughts by composing three test questions. Students distinguish between the general topic of their research and particular details and then express reasons why these facts are important in understanding the course.

A tremendous opportunity achieved by crafting individualized research projects is having older students teach younger ones. These interactions produce intense feelings of confidence and happiness in my students, and I encourage students who produce any child-friendly project: a children's book, model, puppet show, song, painting, or video.

Consider Justine: "I went to present my model of Graceland and again to read my children's book. These two experiences were the most valuable things for me out of anything in any class this entire school year. I would really like to become an elementary school teacher and being able to be in a 'teaching' position at a school, in a class, just like the ones I dream about teaching in, was so valuable. I loved it."

Vince said, "This was a valuable experience to say the least, for I felt as though the children were enthralled with my topic, football, and I came away feeling as if the kids learned a great deal about the subject."

Elementary school students gain encouragement by seeing the application of academic skills at more advanced levels. They see reasons for learning to spell, draw, write, and build. My students gain confidence and encouragement in their academic work. Reporters sometimes cover these events.

Reading Projects

These projects rely on flexibility. In American History classes, during the second quarter, students choose fiction or nonfiction books on any subject in American history from 1840 to 1890 or any book written by an American author living between those years.

I eliminate the temptation to read only short books by basing the assignment on time. For honors students, I require 4 hours each week for four weeks. Thus, 16 hours brings a student into B range. If a slow reader tackles *Roots* but does not finish after reading for 20 hours, he is in the running for an A, depending on the quality of his writing. If a fast reader chooses *Little Women* and finishes in 8 hours, he must continue to read. Options include other books by Alcott, a biography of Alcott, or another Civil War book. If fast readers complain, I say, "Your reward is more knowledge." If slow readers reveal dyslexia, I say, "It's OK to read pages three times."

What makes a book enjoyable and influential varies from person to person. Students write journals based on personal but not private reactions to passages they select. Perhaps they like or dislike a passage. Maybe they don't understand what's going on or look up a historical reference or can relate to a character's thoughts. Students write two such pages each week over the course of four weeks, for a total of eight pages, for a B, depending also on the variety, depth, and quality of their writing.

Reading projects end with polished, four-page typed papers in which students judge the author's expertise, summarize their reading, and explain how it affected them. They deepen their personal reactions from their journals and earn extra credit by producing a poster or by watching a movie or documentary related to their book(s).

Certain types of research projects lend themselves to particular courses. Students in history courses favor children's books, models, paintings, family scrapbooks, persuasive research reports, videos, and reading projects. However, students in other social studies courses often choose specialized projects such as budgets, trips, shadowing, and law or economics in action.

Creative and flexible research projects inspire students to pursue their interests and to showcase their talents. Students gain confidence and have fun while working hard if we guide them skillfully. The results are worth all of our efforts. As you begin to cut chapters and lessons from your yearly practice to make room for these projects, remember Danielle: "If I had to look at another research paper or stereotypical 'research project,' I was going to choke myself. So, I chose to write a children's book because it is a creative project, a fun project. I chose the topic as the structure of the U.S. government because when I learned about checks and balances as a fourth or fifth grader, I thought it was so cool! I wanted to share my fascination with the very age group in which mine started. I thought it would be like coming full circle."

Helpful Tips

Children's Book

1. Leave a blank space on the template for the number of pages with hand-drawn images and text required for a B. Require fewer pages for students in lower grades and for those working alone or in remedial classes. I usually require eight pages from students working alone.

2. Require an annotated bibliography in which students describe their use of three sources and their review of two children's books.

Model

1. If a student chooses a model requiring a high skill level, ask for a time log and award a B for 12 hours of work even if it remains unfinished.

2. Models made from scratch should collapse or fit through doors without tilting.

---

3. Models of weapons should have parental consent and not be operational at school.

Painting

1. Encourage original designs but allow reproductions of highly detailed images.

2. Collages are best because students research images that reveal a topic's import.

Family Scrapbook

1. Focus the scrapbook on three family stories related to the course.

2. Photographs should be labeled with name, date, and location.

3. Require a pedigree chart beginning with the student and extending at least as far back as the participants in the highlighted stories.

4. Do not make any marks in the scrapbook. The student should be confident that the object is to produce a family heirloom.

Persuasive Research Report

1. For one student working alone, I usually require five pages, five sources, and one poster for a B.

2. My juniors and seniors constantly make mistakes when citing sources, so I include examples of Modern Language Association citations on the contract and require students to have their citation methods checked by a media center teacher.

Video

1. One minute of video represents at least an hour of work, making the basis for a B a 12-minute video with five sources.

2. The video should be persuasive and progress with an introduction, analysis of evidence, and conclusion. Negotiate creative exceptions.

3. The video should fit a standard PG rating. Images must be bright and focused, sound should be clear and loud, and editing should be smooth.

4. Students should complete the script by the date of the halfway check.

5. Background music related to the topic enriches videos as much as fancy graphics.

Reading

1. Bring in books you've recently read yourself. Display enthusiasm.

2. Do not limit students to a list of books. Give them freedom.

3. Keep track of books students choose. This gives you titles to suggest and insight into issues concerning each generation of students.

Hybrid or Original Idea

1. Maintain flexibility and openness. Musical performances, handmade costumes, dances, and puppet shows are rare but valid expressions of research and understanding. Allow students to pursue these and other unusual projects.

2. Create a template for a general research project contract with blank spaces for the number of research sources, the length and focus of a written component, details governing the main product, the student's self-evaluation, and your grading notes.

CHAPTER 16

Promoting Citizenship

Teresa Heinhorst

Manito, Illinois

> *The first requisite of a good citizen in this republic of ours is that he shall be able and willing to pull his weight.*
>
> Theodore Roosevelt

Students are taught the meaning \of citizenship in primary and middle school. High school students are given opportunities to be involved in their communities, which can ultimately lead to lifelong participation. Feeling connected to the community gives students pride and a vested interest in seeing the community grow and prosper. As a high school social science teacher, I teach students about government and model behaviors for my students. I am a voting registrar, so I can register every 18-year-old student to vote. We hold mock elections for students to see the voting process directly. I have our county clerk come speak to our students about elections and voting. It is important for students to meet local officials and make positive connections to what they do. There are other ways to seek participation in government for our students.

Teachers may want to seek out different leadership or legislative days in their state. Many legislators have these for schools in their district. Students can meet legislators and participate in government activities. This is quite beneficial. It allows them to hear about current issues and to see these legislators as "real" people. I have taken students on field trips to see our congressman address our local elderly on health care and pharmaceutical costs. The students watch citizens ask some tough questions of the congressman. They see active citizenship modeled by their own local citizens. Involvement in the community is a citizen's responsibility. This needs to be stressed to students when they are in high school.

In the past few years, I have assigned community service responsibilities to my students. When they work in the community, they are making connections with organizations and people they would have never known. It is hoped that these experiences will open the door to their involvement as adults as well. Many students are too self-conscious to attend meetings or events on their own. Encourage a few students to attend a school board meeting or a city council meeting together. As an audience member in these meetings, students will feel confident to attend future meetings, learn about local government, and possibly feel the desire to run for office in the future. We should continually try to make them feel comfortable with government and their role in it.

Every student has an opinion on what is right or wrong in our local, state, or federal government. I assign students to write or e-mail a legislator with an issue they feel strongly about. This may take a day or two of class discussion over topics that interest most students. They may want to write to compliment a legislator on a job well done. I view all letters and e-mails and make suggestions and corrections on how to make their point in a professional and positive manner. They feel personally rewarded when they receive responses. This project teaches students how to assert their opinions effectively. The correspondence gives them a connection to an official and teaches them active citizenship. I have been given the opportunity of a lifetime to teach young people. I take this job very seriously. Not only can we help to make students better citizens, but ultimately their citizenship will lead to a more democratic society. When students are active citizens, they are respectful of adults, and it is reciprocated. The first step to citizenship is to make connections between students and their community.

Helpful Tips

1. Encourage citizenship by having students participate in contests. Many groups, including the VFW and American Legion, have contests, or you can design your own. Find a donor for a prize.

2. Encourage students to be involved in the community. No one turns down help!

3. Work with organizations to place students in appropriate community service positions.

4. Ask local officials to speak to your class.

5. Encourage students to write or e-mail legislators or local politicians.

6. Bring in registrars to encourage voter registration (or become one yourself!).

CHAPTER 17

Reflections From a High School History Teacher

Robert Rodey

Chicago Heights, Illinois

I am finishing my forty-third year of high school teaching, almost all of those years in history. I teach in a team-teaching, interdisciplinary setting. My AP U.S. history classes are actually one-half of an American studies course that integrates U.S. history and English. In American studies, I teach history while my partner prepares the same students for the AP exam in English language and composition. Specifically, he teaches a survey of American literature that parallels my teaching of history. This encourages students to see history and literature as mutually reinforcing. Moreover, the history I teach makes the literature more meaningful, and the literature humanizes the history. Because music and art are components of American studies, I teach a cursory survey of both. I present music in my classroom, and for art we take our students to the Art Institute of Chicago and examine their first-rate American collection. In the following paragraphs, I explain why I maintain my enthusiasm for and effectiveness in teaching high school.

▧ Modified Socratic Method

My most important job is to enable students to see the complexity of history caused by changing historical interpretations as well as the multiple perspectives of the different groups that constitute U.S. history. I use the "on the one hand, but on the other hand" approach. My pedagogy is best described as a modified Socratic method. For example, on a typical day I might begin class with having a student read aloud the preamble to the Constitution. A key phrase from the preamble is "We the People of the United States, in Order to . . . secure the Blessings of Liberty to ourselves and our Posterity, do ordain and establish this Constitution . . ." I then ask another student what this means. After a brief discussion of liberty, I ask, "On the other hand, what does the body of the Constitution say about slavery?" This is a subtle question because the Constitution does not explicitly use the word *slavery*; however, it does recognize slavery through passages that protect certain aspects of slavery. Finally, students come to realize that the original Constitution allows and, more indirectly, actually looks out for the needs of slave owners. Then I ask the big question: How can this be? How can a Constitution dedicated in part to liberty condone slavery? To this question, there is no right or wrong answer, only different perspectives.

During these discussions, I insist on the use of knowledge gained through the required reading as support for students' analyses; I never accept idle speculation. I use "modified" to describe my Socratic method because often I need to interrupt the discussion with didactic teaching. For example, when students discover the "three-fifths compromise" in the Constitution, I teach the census and resulting apportionment of seats in the House of Representatives, using my dry-erase board and black markers.

I teach students how to learn from and participate in class discussions. My seating arrangement is two parallel semicircles, so students can look at each other when they talk. I insist that students make eye contact when talking and call each other by name when making follow-up comments. My job, besides making the didactic contributions I have described, is to keep the discussion going. At the same time, students need to feel confident that if they make a mistake, neither their peers nor I will humiliate them; this is why I need to make my classroom a safe haven from the sometimes intolerant teenage social subculture in schools.

Continuing Professional Development

I learn about historiography and multiple perspectives in summer institutes that I have been attending for years. When I decided that the classroom, not school administration, was the right place for me, I decided to pursue summer institutes for teachers. I have been fortunate to be able to participate in so many of these experiences, most sponsored by the National Endowment for the Humanities. Top professors in the country teach the latest research in history. Last summer, I spent a week studying the Underground Railroad and another week studying Art Deco architecture. Summer institutes have led me to visit Japan, South Korea, Germany, and Cambridge University in the United Kingdom. I have participated in two Gilder Lehrman summer institutes. These experiences have had a profound effect on my teaching. I learn new material and have fresh perspectives to integrate into my class discussions and assigned readings. The summer institutes keep me enthusiastic and motivated. Students ask how I can still be so enthusiastic about teaching after so many years. The answer is that I keep learning and I perceive history as ever more multidimensional.

Classroom Debates

I use debates to teach history. Once or twice a week in each history class, two students debate each other as historical figures, such as Abraham Lincoln versus Stephen Douglas or Alexander Hamilton versus Thomas Jefferson. I insist that students assume the first-person approach and actually "become" their assigned persons. I also insist that they inject passion into their debates so they do not become boring oral reports. As a result, they pound the podium and speak with feeling.

Students learn from one another through debates and learn to disagree as responsible adults. Students are conditioned by their high school subculture to be "cool" and detached in class: only nerds show an actual interest in what the teacher is teaching. That same subculture might condone intensity in their social milieu, but not in response to what a history teacher is directing. It is hoped that in these debates students learn how exciting it is to contest a historical issue, such as "Was the use of two atomic bombs on Japan morally defensible?"

All of the above prepares students to be successful on the AP exam in United States history. I am an ardent supporter of the AP exam because it emphasizes the same approach to history that I use. The ever-closer approaching date of the AP exam is also a marvelous incentive for me to keep the class moving and avoid getting bogged down in a historical period that I personally like. In addition, I love the high standards of the AP exam. Having been an essay grader for the College Board (they supervise the AP exams) for many years, I know how rigorously those exams are graded. At the same time, I take an inclusive attitude toward the nature of the students who enroll in AP U.S. history. I teach close to 120 juniors, which constitutes between one-fourth to one-third of the junior class. Many high schools take a much more selective attitude toward the privileged few who are invited to take an AP class. I reject this elitist approach.

▧ Flexible Lesson Plans

My planning process in all of my classes is rather unique. I do not have a rigid lesson plan completely figured out in advance. For example, on Monday I may begin a class period with the question, "What do you think was the most important program of FDR's New Deal during the 1930s?" The class then proceeds from that single prompt. My first-hour class may answer "Social Security" to that question, which obviously leads to a full discussion of Social Security. Second hour, however, may respond with the Tennessee Valley Authority. My point is that each of my five classes may take a different approach to that same question. At the end of each class, I take a few notes on what we have just covered. Then, as the week progresses, I look back at what I taught in each class. By Thursday or so, I become more directed in my teaching so that by the end of the unit on the Depression, all five classes have received a similar overview of the New Deal.

Because each of my classes resembles a dialogue on the New Deal and the Depression, each takes a different route to what becomes in the end a fairly uniform unit on the New Deal and the Depression; not only are carbon copy outcomes not essential either to students' education or to success on the AP exams, but they are also destructive of any spontaneity and organic development in my teaching. I direct the students to pay attention to relevant primary sources in their textbooks and handouts. Political cartoons, charts, graphs, maps, passages from letters and speeches, and artworks are important to the study of history at the AP level. Because students have difficulty making inferences from primary sources, I guide them through the interpretive process in a clearly directive manner.

Intellectual Inquiry Tempered by Humor

Overall, my classroom teaching is basically teacher centered, but with a sizeable component of student input and direction through discussion. It is also characterized by what I consider to be humanity and intellectual introspection. Finally, to leaven the stress and academic pressure that might emanate from the reading and writing demands of an AP-level course, I use humor to make students more relaxed. The humor that I use is one that comes fairly naturally to me after a lifetime of laughing at Peter Sellers, Mel Brooks, and Monty Python movies. Students seem to appreciate this kind of humor and understand it in the way I intended.

Labeling my teaching style is difficult. Because my classes are teacher directed, to call my teaching style traditional is tempting. I am also not a technocrat. Although I use online resources and encourage students to do the same, especially in their research and AP test preparation, technology doesn't occupy center stage in my classroom. The climate in my classroom is not traditional in the sense of a teacher as the all-knowing answer man who rules with fear and intimidation. Rather, I strive to create a setting characterized by intellectual inquiry in which my students and I are grappling with history together. I know what they need to do on the AP exam to earn high scores (my students do much better than the national average). I am daily humbled by the questions they ask and the insights they share and I am not afraid to admit my lapses.

At the risk of sounding trite, we are all students of history trying our hardest to understand the past. I also do not waste instructional time on what I call "policies." I have strict rules about makeup work, attendance, tardiness, and homework. I avoid creating byzantine, fine-tuned policies about trivial matters. I have met too many teachers who get so bogged down in enforcing their policies that they lose sight of their basic mission: to teach. I do not become so mired in paperwork that I have no life outside of school. To keep myself intellectually active and emotionally healthy, I must have time to read; reflect; go to concerts, plays, and movies; and socialize with friends and family. If teaching history makes me into a miserable, one-dimensional person, what message does that send to students? High school history teaching for me has been a wonderfully satisfying career that is not over yet. If I were given the chance to live my life over again, I would choose teaching.

Index

**CORWIN
PRESS**

The Corwin Press logo—a raven striding across an open book—represents the union of courage and learning. Corwin Press is committed to improving education for all learners by publishing books and other professional development resources for those serving the field of PreK–12 education. By providing practical, hands-on materials, Corwin Press continues to carry out the promise of its motto: **"Helping Educators Do Their Work Better."**